S0-BCT-483

Preface

Many weekends of my childhood were spent with my parents at Islesford, where my mother made a practice of taking me to the Islesford Museum, which she had helped her father to found and develop.

There she would hobnob with curator Paul Eaton, swapping what I sometimes imagined were tall tales about the history of the Cranberry Isles and its people: fishermen who became high-ranking Civil War officers and then returned home to resume fishing; a local man who went out into a snowstorm to fetch a jug of molasses for his wife and returned five years later, molasses in hand; a captain from "the Big Island" who toured the royal cities of Europe with a display of "Esquimeaux" and other artifacts from the Arctic.

I asked to be shown about that last one.

Imagine the late afternoon rays of a summer sun streaming through a west-facing loft window, lighting the dust of the air, a flaw in its old glass focusing a rainbow of hues upon an array of fur-covered trunks, old firearms, swords and furniture under dusty eaves – a small boy's paradise. "Here we are," Mother told me, "These were Sam Hadlock's things, the *God's Pocket* things." And then she sat me down on the dim attic stairs and, as we gazed down through the open doors at the foot of the stairs onto the sunlit lawn below, she told me the long story of Captain Sam Hadlock and the schooner *Minerva*, of the Prussian Woman, of Sammy Sanford and of Rachel Field.

It rained the next day, and to ease my restless disappoint-

God's Pocket

ment she thrust into my hands a battered out-of-print book whose torn cover proclaimed its title – *God's Pocket*. It was the first grown-up book I couldn't put down.

That day in the summer of 1955 I became one of those few dedicated people who believed that Miss Field's story must not be allowed to fade into obscurity. It must be kept alive. The book must be reprinted. Now, thanks to a number of people no less convinced than I, here it is.

The Islesford Historical Society, the Northeast Harbor Library and the Cranberry Isles Historical Society would like to thank the Trustees of Radcliffe College and the estate of Arthur S. Pederson for permission to reprint *God's Pocket*. We are grateful to Carl Little for his excellent and scholarly new introduction; to Hugh Dwelley for his informative afterward; to Edwin Chase of Studio 3, who guided us from start to finish; to Gunnar Hansen for his help and guidance; to Acadia National Park's William Otis Sawtelle Collections and Research Center and Brooke Childrey, its curator, for help and permission to use materials from the Islesford museum; to Louise Sawtelle Libby, who helped keep her father's and Miss Field's torches of scholarship alight through the lean years of waning interest; and most of all to O. P. Jackson, Jr., who made possible the realization of a dream shared by us all – to tell again the amazing story.

Robert R. Pyle
June 1999

ii

Introduction

Rachel Field: An Appreciation

I

Novelist, poet, playwright and writer of children's books, Rachel Lyman Field was born in New York City in 1894. The family moved to Stockbridge, in western Massachusetts, following the death of Rachel's father in 1895, and then to Springfield when she was ten. Later in life, she stated that, had she had her way, she would have been born in Maine. (On another occasion, she wrote, "I consider myself a New Englander. For example, I do not put tomatoes in chowder. I make the white kind.")

Field came from a line of distinguished men of the world, including her father's three esteemed uncles: Cyrus Field, who laid the first trans-Atlantic cable; David Dudley Field, who developed international codes of legal procedure; and Justice Stephen J. Field of the United States Supreme Court.

Unable to meet the entrance requirements in mathematics, Field attended Radcliffe University in 1914-1918, the four war years, as a "special student"; her excellence in writing helped her gain acceptance (she claims to have learned to write before she could read). There she took George Pierce Baker's renowned English 47 course for budding playwrights (other graduates included Eugene O'Neill and Thomas Wolfe). She had her first writing success in the theater, win-

God's Pocket

ning the Drama League of America prize in 1918 for "Rise Up, Jennie Smith." Another play, "Three Pills in a Bottle," was produced at Radcliffe and became popular with theater groups across the country.

After college Field spent six years in her native city writing synopses of plays and books for Famous Players-Lasky, producers of silent motion pictures. At the same time she was writing verse, short plays and a novel, but publishers took little interest. A few editors, however, admired her evocations of childhood.

This encouragement led to her second success, as an author of children's books. Her first book, *The Pointed People*, was published by the Yale University Press ("I had the misfortune to have it come out the year A.A. Milne's *When We Were Very Young* was sweeping the country," she later recalled).

In 1929, *Hitty: Her First One Hundred Years* won for its author the Newbery Medal for the most distinguished contribution to children's literature, the first ever awarded to a woman (it was also the first prize book with an American background). Also chosen as one of the best fifty books of 1929 by the Typographical Society of America, *Hitty*, which recounts the adventures of a doll made of mountain ashwood, has remained in print to this day.

Field always gave equal credit for the success of *Hitty* to

iv

her collaborator, the illustrator Dorothy P. Lathrop. While the author self-illustrated a number of her own children's books (sometimes with her skilled cut-outs), she also had the great fortune to have some of the masters of the day—Lathrop, Allen Lewis, Elizabeth MacKinstry and Ilse Bischoff, among others—render her stories into pictures.

Children's natures, Field once observed, "do not change perceptibly from one generation to another. It is their dress, their speech and their manners that change, not their natures." She criticized writers who wrote down to children, employing words "so simplified that all the spirit is lost in commonplaces." She followed Irish dramatist J.M. Synge's advice regarding dialogue: "Every phrase should be finely flavored as a nut or an apple."

Field also gained popularity and renown for her novels. In 1938 she produced a bestseller, *All This, and Heaven Too*, a fictionalized account of her great-aunt who had been the famous "Mademoiselle D." of Paris, a central figure in the de Praslin murder case (she married the Reverend Henry M. Field and moved to America). This book was made into a movie by Warner Brothers in 1940, starring Bette Davis and Charles Boyer; Field had an opportunity to watch some of the filming.

Two other Field novels received Hollywood treatment:

God's Pocket

And Now Tomorrow, Paramount Pictures, 1944, with Loretta Young and Alan Ladd; and *Time Out of Mind*, United Artists, 1947, starring Phyllis Calvert and Robert Hutton. The latter book, published in 1935, received the first-ever National Book Award for the most distinguished novel of the year, presented by Christopher Morley on behalf of the American Booksellers Association. Set in Bucksport, Maine, *Time Out of Mind* evokes the last days of the clipper ships.

In and among these award winners and best sellers were numerous collections of plays and poems. Field also compiled fairy and folk tales and on occasion illustrated other writers' works. *People from Dickens*, 1935, presented leading characters from the books of the great English writer; and she wrote new lyrics for "Ave Maria" for the concluding number of Walt Disney's Fantasia. She also was a gifted and loyal correspondent. One of her letters to her mother, recounting a meeting with J.M. Barrie, author of *Peter Pan*, was printed in *The Horn Book*.

In 1935, at the age of thirty-nine, Field married Arthur Pederson, a literary agent; after a honeymoon in Maine, they moved to Beverly Hills. The Pedersons collaborated on a novel about Hollywood, *To See Ourselves*, published in 1937. They adopted a daughter, Hannah, in 1939. Field died at the Good Samaritan Hospital in Los Angeles on March 15,

God's Pocket

1943, at age forty seven, succumbing to cancer following an operation and a brief illness. She is buried in Stockbridge.

II

And because he entrusted his grandfather's story to me, I can only hope that I of a different time, who came so far to hear it, shall not fail in the telling.

Rachel Field, *God's Pocket*

Nearly every summer, from age 15 on, Field accompanied her family to Sutton Island, one of the five Cranberry Isles. She would later state that the island meant "roots and background" to her; "and I suppose that it, more than any one other thing in my life, has helped me with my writing." She eventually purchased "The Playhouse" on Sutton with the royalties from her first book of plays.

The Cranberries became a major source of material for Field, inspiring what is perhaps her most popular piece of writing, the poem, "If Once You Have Slept On an Island," which first appeared in *St. Nicholas Magazine* in the mid-1920s. "There's something about islands," she once said. "I don't know what it is, but I simply cannot keep them out of the things I write. I always find them there along with pointed trees, toadstools, children and patchwork quilts."

God's Pocket

Visiting the islands in the early part of this century, Field had the opportunity to witness firsthand the life of the islanders. Among her books that include depictions of the Cranberries is *Points East: Narratives of New England*, first published in 1930. This collection of "old, incredibly convincing tales," as one contemporary reviewer described it, represented the author's first volume written exclusively for adults.

Field also wrote about the islands in her acclaimed *Calico Bush*, 1931, which was a Newbery Medal Honor Book and is still in print. Here the author ventured to write a fictional chronicle of the Cranberry Isles' earliest settlers, as seen through the eyes of Marguerite Ledoux, a French girl bound out to a family from Marblehead, Massachusetts. The story took its inspiration from the life of Margarita LaCroix, who lived on Maypole Point on Little Cranberry Island in the second half of the 18th century.

Perhaps Field's greatest downeast book was *God's Pocket*, published in 1934, "The Story," so reads its subtitle, "of Captain Samuel Hadlock, Junior of Cranberry Isles, Maine." Field had been given Captain Hadlock's journal by his grandson and namesake, Samuel Sanford (1852-1933). From this source and Sanford's own accounts of his grandfather, the author pieced together a most remarkable tale, a hybrid of

God's Pocket

sorts, called by its publisher "a biographical novel." A good portion of the book recounts the travels of Captain Hadlock in Europe, England, Scotland and Ireland. For four years the Cranberry Islander roamed among Old World cities with his sideshow, which consisted of an Eskimo couple, who performed fishing, hunting and other Native American skills, and a collection of artifacts – "Genuine Indians and curiosities from the shores of North America" is how the P.T. Barnumesque Hadlock billed his show. They entertained at fairs, in small villages, and for royalty in palace gardens.

While visiting Charlottenburg, outside of Berlin, Captain Hadlock became smitten with a Prussian woman, Dorethea Albertina Wilhelmina Celeste Russ, and courted and married her. Unable to pronounce his wife's name, Hadlock called her Hannah Caroline.

Throughout her account of Hadlock's journeys, Field never loses sight of her subject's ties to his home country. Writing about his love for Dorethea/Hannah, she likens his passion to "the sudden vehemence of spring in northern Maine":

> I know how the ice breaks with dull thunder; how the barriers go down in a single night; how arbutus and violets spring from melting snows, and a green, fiercer than flame, runs over brown pastures and

ix

God's Pocket

ledges. No soft, slowly unfolding southern spring ever was so charged with the enduring passions of earth.

Soon after the couple's daughter, Jane Matilda, was born, they set sail for Great Cranberry Island. One of the most moving sections of *God's Pocket* occurs in Chapter XVII, where Field relates the return of Captain Hadlock and his Prussian bride to Maine in 1826. More than perhaps anywhere else in the book, the author here interjects her personal feelings toward the Maine coast.

Not knowing the actual route the couple took, Field has them follow her ideal passage down east. "I like to think," she muses, "that it was one of those incredible summer mornings of hot sea-sunshine and a breeze with the faintest hint of ice in it, when they saw the hills of Mount Desert come up over the port bows, dim at first, like sea-bound whales, but gradually taking shape into the nine hump-backed hills that dominate the sea and land for many miles."

Their approach to the island echoes the sense of wonder found in an equally memorable passage in *Calico Bush* when Marguerite Ledoux first catches sight of Mount Desert Island in the distance:

And then, suddenly, as Marguerite stood at the wooden rail, her eyes shaded against the brightness, a miracle of mountains came out of the sea. Like dim, blue monsters swimming away from land they loomed to the northeast.

God's Pocket abounds in such felicities of description. One also admires the way Field turns the image of the pocket into a powerful leit-motif. "You're as safe with me as if you was in God's pocket," Sammy Sanford tells the narrator early in the book. About mid-way, we come across this statement: "To have stepped at thirty, in the vigor of self-assured young manhood, from a remote pocket of the new world into the age-mellowed cities of an older civilization, must have stimulated a far less imaginative man than Samuel Hadlock." And then there is that final "dark pocket," the hole in the ice through which the "Esquimaux" lower Hadlock's frozen body.

In his *Biography of an Island*, 1958, Perry D. Westbrook noted that "Most outstanding [of islander characteristics], and most often celebrated in novels of the Maine coast, is a highly developed sense of independence." The great Maine writer Edward Holmes underscores this notion in his essay "What Should Maine Writers Write?" 1962. "If Maine writers tend to portray, not the college-groomed suburbanite, but the individualist, the oddball of the coastal village or forest," he wrote, "this is more of a compliment than anything else. One does not always find such people so readily in every state."

God's Pocket

Field's life of Samuel Hadlock stands in a line of portraits of self-reliant Maine coast men that would include Charles Eliot's *John Gilley: One of the Forgotten Millions*, 1899, Edwin Day Sibley's *Stillman Gott, Farmer and Fisherman*, 1902, and Francis Greenwood Peabody's portrait of Frederick Illsley Phillips, a Mount Desert fisherman, schoolteacher and farmer, in *Lives of Present-Day Saints*, 1927.

Hadlock, Gilley, Gott and Phillips appear larger than life. They are clearly admired by their portrayers, yet they receive honest rendering (in this way, these figures presage Carolyn Chute's *Beans of Egypt, Maine*). Field, for example, treats Hadlock with respect, but she confirms his faults. The unlearned English that he wrote in his journal, for instance, is carefully reproduced by Field (Louise Libby once remarked that the journals had to be translated "since Sam couldn't spell for sour apples"). Here's an example of his crude spelling, from a description of the Fourth of July:

> Evereay true sitison of Columbias hapey land shood bair in mind and remember on that day she shook off the yoke of a tiranikall government and fread hurself of many Imbarissments that iss imposed on her mother cuntrey.

Like Mary Ellen Chase and other historical writers of New England, Field has suffered over the years from critical

God's Pocket

neglect. She is conspicuously absent from a number of anthologies, including the otherwise excellent *Maine Speaks*, 1989. Granted her novels are not easily excerpted, yet earlier compilations, such as Henry Beston's *White Pine and Blue Water*, 1950, and W. Storrs Lee's *Maine: A Literary Chronicle*, 1968, found room for her.

Why this neglect? One supposes that it is the "old-fashioned" nature of Field's prose, the wonderful flourishes that date it to another era. And perhaps she has fallen victim to a certain "correctness" that disapproves of tales of exploitation. (I remember happening upon a reader's guide to books about Native Americans, in which it was suggested that Field's *Calico Bush* be avoided because she used the word "Injun." No consideration was made of the author's seamless prose or of the fact that such usage, as in the novels of Mark Twain, provides a perfect opportunity to discuss prejudice with young readers.)

The novel has had its champions. Reviewing Field's skills as a writer, Stephen Vincent Benet wrote that she "had a gift for the past and the honest things of the past—it shows in *Hitty*, perhaps the best loved of her children's books, as it does in that wise and true little book *God's Pocket*."

The reprinting of *God's Pocket* after more than fifty years in a state of more or less limbo (stashed away in the rare book

xiii

sections of libraries or the shelves of summer island homes) marks the start of what this writer hopes will be a Rachel Field revival. A call for a reprint has been in the air since the author's death: "...the material for the book swam luminous out of a Maine fog and it remains in *God's Pocket* as her truest adult book," Josiah Titzell wrote in *The Horn Book* in 1943. "Too few know it now as at the time of its publication too few knew it."

Now, happily, *God's Pocket* is back in circulation and many more readers will have the opportunity to know it.

Carl Little

Carl Little has written extensively on the art and literature of the Maine coast. His essays have appeared in a range of periodicals, including The Island Journal, The Bar Harbor Times *and the* Journal of the Mount Desert Historical Society. *His most recent book is* Art of the Maine Islands.

God's Pocket

Notes

An exhibit devoted to Field and her island writings can be found in the Islesford Historical Museum on Little Cranberry Island, Maine.

The author thanks Phoebe White Wentworth for supplying material that proved invaluable to the writing of this essay. Key texts include: *The Horn Book*, special Rachel Field memorial issue, July 1942; *Something About the Author*, volume 15, pp. 106-113 (includes comprehensive bibliography); *Junior Book of Authors*, pp. 148-151; "Rachel Field of the Cranberry Isles," by Herbert Edwards, *Down East*, August 1971; Who Was Who, pp. 614-615 (entry written by Cornelia Meigs); obituary, *New York Times*, March 16, 1942; *Library Journal*, July, 1930, p. 603. The author also drew on transcripts of interviews conducted by Sheila Polson.

God's Pocket

THE MACMILLAN COMPANY
NEW YORK · BOSTON · CHICAGO · DALLAS
ATLANTA · SAN FRANCISCO

MACMILLAN & CO., LIMITED
LONDON · BOMBAY · CALCUTTA
MELBOURNE

THE MACMILLAN COMPANY
OF CANADA, LIMITED
TORONTO

God's Pocket

The Story of
Captain Samuel Hadlock, Junior
of Cranberry Isles, Maine

By Rachel Field

But so it is. Experience, like the stern lanthorn of a ship, casts its light only on the wake—on the track already past.

—S. T. COLERIDGE

New York

The Macmillan Company

1934

To

The Memory
of
Samuel C. Sanford
Cranberry Isles, Maine
1852–1933

Acknowledgment

For his help in supplementing this word-of-mouth story, I am indebted to William O. Sawtelle, who put the documents relating to Samuel Hadlock and his family in the Islesford Museum Collection at my disposal, and who also gave me the benefit of his years of research into the history of the Cranberry Isles.

For the text of the ballad on "The Loss of the Schooner Minerva," *and other details of the 1829 sealing expedition, I am also indebted to Miss Mary W. Smyth, who assembled the Island songs in* Minstrelsy of Maine, *by Fannie H. Eckstorm and Mary W. Smyth, published by the Houghton Mifflin Co. in 1927.*

And to Mrs. Rose Wedge and Mrs. John Hamor of Big Cranberry I am grateful for their personal recollections of "The Prussian Lady."

God's Pocket

God's Pocket

Chapter I

"And he stoppeth one of three . . ."—S. T. COLERIDGE.

NOTHING remains of him now but a gold snuffbox; a silhouette cut in London in 1824; an old compass, maps, and a chart; a marriage certificate in German script, and two tattered copy books crowded with faded entries in a vigorous Spencerian hand. These, and a story of romantic enterprise and love and tragedy that has quickened my mind since I first heard mention of Captain Samuel Hadlock, Jr., of Cranberry Isles.

No one living now can remember him or that morning in 1829 when he took command of the ill-fated *Minerva* and its crew of Maine men, his relatives and neighbors. No one alive today saw her put out between the familiar islands, heading for northern waters and ice floes. But I have talked with those who saw the Prussian Lady in their youth, who can vouch for the

1

legend that she was the prettiest woman on any of the islands. They remember the foreign ways and furbelows she brought with her across the Atlantic, from a country she was never to see again. I have held the London silhouette in my hands, and I know Samuel Hadlock's profile as if it were a near neighbor's.

He was thirty-two years old when the artist cut it from the dark red paper, and touched the wavy hair and upstanding fur collar with flecks of gilt paint. But the bold, humorous nose, the full lips, the firm chin, and the proud set of the head need no such embellishing. Vigor and fearlessness are in every feature. This was the State of Maine showman in the heyday of his fortunes, when he exhibited his pair of Indians all over England and the Continent and hobnobbed familiarly with Kings and Queens in their palaces. This is how he looked when he drove his coach and horses to Dresden and Munich, to Vienna and Prague and Paris, setting down his doings and impressions of foreign folks and fashions in the copy books that lie open before me as I write.

Many of the pages are missing, and it was more than a dozen years before these few came into my hands. I can remember just how and when I first heard the story from his grandson and namesake, Samuel Sanford, whose mother was born to Hadlock and the Prussian Lady in Paris, two years after the silhouette was cut. I had seen the old man several times, walking alone on the road or along the shore of Big Cranberry Island. He

2

was one of those gaunt, spare old men who somehow contrive to grow into a very counterpart of the place they inhabit. We did not exchange greetings, and when he hailed me suddenly across a wild raspberry patch by a certain sheltered back cove one afternoon in July, I felt as startled as if the Ancient Mariner had stopped me.

But there was no strange glitter to his mild blue eyes in their nests of wrinkles. His voice was soft, and he spoke with a curious grave precision that made what he said seem all the more unreal as I listened. I can remember his very words, and that we sat together in the open door of an old fish house set between crowding spruces and a pebble beach. The hills of Mount Desert showed humped and dark across the wide blue waters of the Western Way, as they may have looked the day Captain Samuel Hadlock set off with his arctic curiosities for far parts; as they must have looked often to the Prussian Lady those years she waited for news of the *Minerva*.

A clutter of lobster traps, old nets, and buoys lay at our feet, with purple wild beach-pea vines climbing over and about them. Gulls littered the water about a fishing boat anchored near by. The tide was in, and the small cove so full of sea that the spruces on the sheltering point were almost wading in their own reflections. The village with its store and post office and neat houses set along the road might have been far away though it was only a scant half-mile behind us. Even time, ticking in the watch on my wrist, seemed to have no part in the stillness of the Back Cove or the story that years could not dull or rob of its compelling power.

I wondered then and I wonder now, why the old man should have called me out of the berry patch for his audience that summer afternoon. I was in my early twenties, and the past had not yet laid hold upon me. He must have been well to the northward of seventy, and the present could have made few demands upon him beyond his own daily needs. But there we were, caught for an hour in one of those timeless intervals when the past is linked to the present by the frail thread of a human voice.

"Don't be frightened," I remember he said to me, as his grandfather may have reassured the Prussian Lady years before. "You're as safe with me as if you was in God's pocket."

I have always treasured the phrase. It seemed to belong to that northern cove and the loves and journeyings and strange enterprises of an Island man in that small pocket of Eternity which each of us fills for a lifetime.

And now old Sammy is dead, too, buried beside his mother and the Prussian Lady in the cemetery at Southwest Harbor. His little house is empty, and his garden already going to seed.

It was late last July when I visited him and heard the story once again from his own lips. The afternoon was fine and sunny after a spell of rain, and I had gone with a friend to call on him. He looked older and more frail than I remembered. As he came out of the spruce wood to greet us, his spare body, his brown face and white hair made me think suddenly of the great pasture thistles after a winter of bleaching. We followed him into the little house that fitted him like his own weathered shell.

Shafts of late sunlight streamed in at the two windows on the carefully spread patchwork quilt that covered the old bunk; on the brass-bound compass that had gone with his grandfather to far ports. The plain, small room was spotless with one man's tending. There was a completeness and order that gave importance to the place; that was strangely touching as I noted each object. Two freshly washed union suits and a gray cotton shirt were hung to dry behind the stove. I marveled at this personal care, knowing as I did that the old man had carried the water in heavy pails from the nearest well half a mile away, and that he had heated it in the big black iron kettle before he could do his washing. How he contrived at all on the few dollars he made from his vegetable garden on a corner of the land that had once belonged to the Hadlock family, no one on the Island knew. But cleanliness and order and dignity were his inheritance. Even in the cheap, washed-out shirt and worn trousers that he had grown too thin to fill, he looked the Island aristocrat that he knew himself to be. His well kept beard was white as a gull's breast, and I caught him smoothing the sparse side locks on his forehead while he talked of his Grandfather Hadlock.

I think I knew, without knowing that I knew, that this would be our last visit together. So I asked him many questions about that European journey; about the Esquimaux and that incredible foreign courtship. He seemed anxious to talk of them, and when he spoke of "Grandfather" and "Grandmother" it was as if a halfgrown boy were speaking and not the eighty-one-yearold man sitting beside us.

Birds were all about his door—song and white-throat sparrows, and juncos, tame because of the crumbs he fed them. They sang in the sunshine just outside, and the incoming tide shuffled the pebbles in the cove beyond the spruces. They seemed to belong to all he said; to be the right and fitting accompaniment to the story.

Just before we rose to go, he brought out a brown paper case and put it in my hands. In it were the two old copy books that held his Grandfather Hadlock's Journal. He had shown them to me before, but I had never been allowed to touch them.

"You can take it back with you," he said. When I protested, he added, "Keep it as long as you want to."

Two days later he was dead. Neighbors from the village found him so, alone. When they told me, I knew that it was as it should be. He belonged alone with the past, and he had had his grandfather's compass and

6

God's Pocket

chart beside him. I knew, too, that he had lived just long enough to put the Journal in my hands. Perhaps that was why he had written in pencil across the torn covers:

This was my Grandfather Hadlock
S. C. Sanford

And because he entrusted his grandfather's story to me, I can only hope that I of a different time, who came so far to hear it, shall not fail in the telling.

Chapter II

"And the place thereof . . ."—Psalms.

SAMUEL HADLOCK and his four brothers were Island-born and had been bred to boats from the cradle. They could handle oars and sails almost before they were out of petticoats, and courses and currents and rocky channels were familiar to them as roads and footpaths to inland boys. Their father, the elder Samuel, built vessels, stout fishing boats and schooners, in the sheltered Pool at Big Cranberry. Here at low tide the water runs out till even a dory is stranded in the wide empty basin. But at high tide quite a sizable vessel may be floated out into the deeper channel between Fish Point and neighboring Little Cranberry. The Pool is almost deserted now; only a few scattered houses and fish sheds edge its shores. It is quiet except for an occasional summer launch or chugging lobster boat, and the cries of gulls and a solitary heron. But in the early eighteen hundreds it was busy with the beat of hammers on sturdy hulls of native timber. The *Cashier*, the *Village Belle*,

8

God's Pocket

the *Dolly*, the *Maypole*, and the *Minerva*—these and others with long forgotten names went out from Cranberry Pool to anchor in Liverpool and Bordeaux and Hamburg; to carry cargoes of salt fish and timber, and to fetch back merchandise, rum, and sugar from the West Indies, or furs from the coast of Greenland.

Even to those familiar with this part of the coast of Maine, it may seem strange that it was from Cranberry Pool and not from the larger ports of Mount Desert that these vessels sailed. Today the five Cranberry Isles —Sutton, Bear, Baker's, Big and Little Cranberry—are less well known than Bar Harbor and the other ports of the larger island. But long before Mount Desert became a popular summer resort, these outer islands, lying scattered between it and open sea, were the more prosperous and thickly settled. It was easier to get and keep a foothold in days when Indians still came down on marauding expeditions from Canada, and when roads were few and boats and waterways served instead of coach and turnpike.

The Indian menace was well past and the American Revolution safely over when Samuel Hadlock, Jr., was born on Little Cranberry. His father's family were well established there in the late seventeen hundreds, but most of his life is bound to the larger Cranberry Island. Except for a few summer cottages, an occasional car on the dirt road that runs across the middle, from western to eastern tip, and the line of telegraph and electric

9

light poles that march beside it, Big Cranberry still looks much as it must have looked when he was living there. The islands of this little northerly group are all small as acreage goes. Even this largest of the five has only 850 acres all told, and this in rough pasture, wooded, and half-cleared land. The pointing firs and spruces still crowd down to the tide-line in bristling ranks of thick-set green. It is a continual fight, as it has always been, to keep them from taking every hard-won field and garden. The shores are sharp and rocky; the few beaches, shifting and pebbled. Apple trees are tough and crooked with straining against sea winds. Lilac bushes bear their bloom on stunted branches. But the wild cranberries that have given the islands their name are bright underfoot in late summer, spicy and delicious as the larger marsh ones can never be. Samuel Hadlock must have eaten them often in his mother's kitchen, and relished them as the grandsons and granddaughters of his old neighbors do today.

This was the place that he grew up in, though he had touched at many ports of the Caribbean before he was halfway through his twenties. His father and brothers were as much at home there as in the familiar waters of Somes' Sound or Frenchman's Bay, and he went with them. But it was always to the more northerly waters that Samuel Hadlock, Jr., sailed alone, and to which he returned again and again. It was as if the Arctic had marked him in youth for its own. Frozen harbors, ice-

God's Pocket

bergs, and snowy wastes had power over him. He could never stay long away. So, while his father and brothers prospered in the West Indies and coast trade, he kept to his sealing and whaling in the far north. Strange cargoes he brought back on those homeward trips— arctic treasures of carved bone; Esquimau spears and harpoons; outlandish dresses of fur and feathers; stuffed seals and bear and northern birds; wonders to widen the eyes of Bunkers and Stanleys, of Spurlings, Bulgers, Gotts, and Gilleys and other Island relatives and friends.

A unique collection it must have been, for Samuel Hadlock had an eye for curiosities. Whether it was a white seal, or rocks in the Giants' Causeway, or a French girl who could work miracles, Samuel Hadlock's imagination quickened at any deviation from the human or natural pattern. From a boyish hobby, this grew into a passion which would not let him settle down to life ashore and the less hazardous ways of fishing and farming. It was like a deep fever in him, an urge that might lie dormant for months and even years, only to break out in a consuming fire. At such times nothing could hold him, not even his wife and children and the Island whose wild strength and meager beauty were so much a part of him.

Perhaps this very restlessness, this inexhaustible energy and curiosity, gave him peculiar power over people, for he had his way wherever he went. Neighbors and Esquimaux, Kings and Queens and rogues—all fell under the spell of his personal magnetism, and no woman could resist his charm.

He had married early, like most Island boys. That was in 1812, when he was twenty and his bride nineteen. She was Amah Richardson of Bass Harbor on the then sparsely settled larger island of Mount Desert. He must have courted her by water, sailing those half-dozen miles across the Western Way. But of these nine years and their life together, there is little to tell, save for the recorded births of three children: Samuel Taylor in 1814; Sally in 1815, and Smith Cobb in 1819. This first marriage seems like an early incident, scarcely remembered in the romantic love for Dorethea Albertina Wilhelmina Celeste which was to sweep him off his feet in Charlottenburg, Prussia, thirteen years after.

If Amah Richardson Hadlock had not died and left him a widower at twenty-nine he might not have taken his curiosities and the Esquimaux to far parts. Perhaps he would have gone anyway. Samuel Hadlock was never one to let a wife and family ties keep him from any enterprise, once it was conceived in his active brain. At any rate he went, shedding the past as easily as a snake slips out of its old skin. Even the other inhabitants of Big Cranberry, used as they were to his roving, daredevil ways, must have thought he had taken leave of his senses. To turn his three young children over to a married sister; to take his entire savings and set off across the Atlantic with his collection of oddities and a pair of Esquimaux from the Arctic Circle—this was surely the most crack-brained of all his exploits thus far. Tongues must have wagged from one end of the Island to the other.

The Esquimaux could hardly have been cordially received in any such small, strait-laced community. Stuffed seals and carved bone and tusks were one thing, but such an outlandish, gibberish-speaking pair, with a little papoose that they had had without being properly married, most likely—they were another matter. Sam Hadlock had better have left them where they belonged. So the Island women must have told each other, not unaware that their husbands and brothers and sons eagerly flocked to inspect the couple, and see for themselves the feats the Esquimau man could perform in a canoe just off-shore. But Samuel Hadlock needed no neighborly encouragement, and so he set off on his travels, as proud as any captain in command, with the world for his quarter-deck.

Chapter III

I took my power in my hand
And went against the world;
'Twas not so much as David had,
But I was twice as bold.
            —EMILY DICKINSON.

MY STORY must begin in the year 1822 with the earliest entry in Samuel Hadlock's European Journal, set down shortly before his thirtieth year.

Where they sailed from and what ship carried him and his Esquimaux to Liverpool, we do not know. But he must have landed there, for Chester is the first entry in his Journal. One can imagine the six-feet Yankee strolling through the streets of that old city, with the strange pair at his heels, and gaping citizens following their progress. We know, because he set down the words himself, that he marveled at those narrow streets with their sagging houses, under whose projecting upper stories pedestrians might walk and do business secure from the weather, or "under kuver" as he puts it. The Roman wall caught his fancy, and he notes that a coach

14

and four may drive in comfort along the top. No wonder such antiquities aroused the admiration of a man who had probably never seen any building more than fifty or seventy-five years old.

It must have been in Chester at some stationer's shop that he bought the marble-backed blank book, and no doubt it was at the Boar's Head, the Royal Arms, or the Crown and Rose, or some other forgotten inn that he dipped a new quill pen in ink to write the record of his doings. That ink is still black, though the handmade paper is almost coffee-colored. The letters are bold and free on the page before me, set down by the steady hand of a confident and self-assured man. He must have practiced his pothooks in Island copy books to make such fine capitals, and to give such a sure, firm slant to the letters; but the spelling is as free of rules and regulations as Samuel Hadlock's own unhindered spirit. Although the same word may be spelled three different ways in a single paragraph, there is a certain consistency once one has mastered his phonetic method of spelling, and he is almost as lavish as Chaucer with his final e's and double consonants. From such a spontaneous document as this one gets a rather different notion of the speech of these earlier New England seacoast men. We have grown so used to clipped g's and a's that it is surprising to find them here given their full value. Certain Yankeeisms occasionally creep in, but for the most part it is the good, vigorous English

15

that seventeenth and eighteenth century settlers brought with them. "Thay ware not so wall skild [skilled] at bulding," he writes of Chester's architecture, "as thay are know [now]." Here is the English "ware" instead of "were," and a broader *a* throughout than we hear in most American speech today.

Hadlock was saving of space in his Journal unless he encountered something out of the ordinary which he felt compelled to set down in detail, and, like New Bedford and Nantucket whalers in their log-book notes, he entered his own exploits briefly. Almost uniformly the mates of whaling ships used two words to record their catch. They never failed to put down the exact time and position where they were when a whale was sighted. They mentioned latitude and longitude and winds and the number of boats that put out after it. But of the chase itself, of the hours spent and the struggle that went into the whale's capture, there was scarcely ever more than the terse phrase, "Got him." So it is with Samuel Hadlock and his exhibiting of the Esquimaux. "Dun Wall," or "Dun torible wall" is his usual comment, with only a rare entry giving the amount of his receipts. What prompted him to write were differences on the face of the earth: the strange looks or customs of the people he encountered; above all any wonder, scenic or human, as the case might be.

It is the town of Holywell in the north of Wales and the legend concerning the well of St. Winifred there that first inspired him to write more than five full pages and to compose a poem in honor of that seventh century miracle. After describing the scenery, the wild hills and valleys, and "the venerable abbey near which terminates that anchent and notable divishion of England and Wales," he launches into a long account of the Holy Well and the story of that "vergin of extrodenary Santity of the name of Winford." He tells how she made a vow of chastity and early dedicated herself to the service of God; of how she was put under the care of her Uncle Beuno in his church; and of how a neighboring heathen Prince named Caradoc "was struck by hur oncomen buty" and "determined to gratify his desires." So, the Journal relates, "he made known his passions to hur who effected with horror atempted hur escape." Winifred's fate at the hands of her wooer is described in full—how his saber cut off her head and how it rolled down to the very door of her uncle's church. He tells then of the double miracle—how Caradoc was struck dead and instantly swallowed up by the earth, while Beuno, carrying the severed head back to the body and offering prayers, saw the two join and the Virgin return to life. He tells of the miraculous healing power of the waters of a spring which burst forth from the place where the head had rested on the moss, and which ever after diffused a fragrant smell. "Hur blod spotted the stones," he writes, "which lik the flowers of Adonis annully commemerating the facts by assuming a collar [color] unknone to them before." The classical allusion is startling in this straightforward account. How Samuel Hadlock had heard of Adonis on remote Cranberry Island will always be an enigma. But it is characteristic that he should have, for it is this unexpected touch of poetry in a shrewd, practical man of business that gives such color and diversity to the Journal.

He thought much, and of necessity, in terms of dollars and cents, but his mind was also a queer repository of the weird and mysterious. He treasured the fabulous of all times and places. Like his spells of restlessness and far-seeking curiosity, this poetical strain cropped out in him whenever a sight or incident could quicken his fancy. Other New England travelers of his day may have possessed this trait, but for the most part they had too much natural restraint to give it full rein. It is rare to find a man unself-conscious enough to admit the wonders that moved him, much less one to set them down on paper.

Samuel Hadlock was a showman and captain by profession, but he saw no reason for not attempting a poem on St. Winifred once the spirit had moved him. So, after further accounts of the famous well, the volume of water in exact tonnage which flowed daily into the basin where travelers came to bathe; the methods of sanitation employed, and the alleged cures of various diseases by means of its healing properties, he lets rhyme have its way with him. At first glance the following verses seem crude and meandering. The influence of hymnal phraseology is apparent, yet the more one reads them the more one is amazed at their vigor and imagery.

> See the watters ever floing
> fresh from hur sacred gore
> Virgines mereth shoing
> A thousen yeres and more
> Fair life and precious helth
> Adorn these living Springes
> Without them whats all welth
> of princes lordes and kinges
> Ye British muses aid the lay
> the Winfordes shall rise
> Over the well and all the way
> Singing eternal joyes
> See faith divine and holy grace
> the fairest progeny of heven
> Enclose the lustres of that plase
> With many helps and blessings given
> the Silver Stremes shall cese to flow
> the hory ocens role
> the graves to sing the flowers to grow
> the stones desert the pole
> While Winfordes shall live
> Beyond the blasts of time
> the mouldering rokes survay
> the hours of our Clime.

God's Pocket

The poem achieved, he easily dismisses the lusters of Holywell, the blasts of time, and St. Winifred herself. "I have now finished my Remarkes concerning this moste noble well," he concludes, "and also the lines that I composed on the Vergin of Gratitude and then I left this most noble citty and traveld to different partes of this Kingdom." Once more he was concerned with practical affairs. The time had come to start his Exhibition.

Chapter IV

From Greenland's icy mountains . . .

IT is strange that the Journal should make such scanty mention of the Esquimaux themselves, for they and their exploiter must have come to know one another intimately in those months and years of travel together. No doubt they became such a part of Samuel Hadlock's life that he took them more or less for granted along with his other charges and responsibilities. What part of the north they hailed from, and what they were like in age and personal appearance, we shall never know. There is no actual reference to the papoose, though I have been assured that there was one.

Of the pair the woman is a clearer personality to me because I have seen an old wood-engraving of her. It hung on the wall of the little house on Cranberry Island and old Sammy often pointed it out to me. The features show only very dimly now, for it was rescued from a fire, and has been much damaged by smoke. But

21

even so, the broad, dark face with a headdress of feathers and heavy ropes of beads, looks out of the frame with dignity and patience and native grace that is all the more appealing in the light of what happened to her. She was called, if I remember rightly, Mary, or Mamie, Megunticook. Whether this was her real name or a fancy one concocted by Hadlock for show purposes, I do not know. He was capable of changing names if they did not suit his pleasure. But all that is certain is that neither she nor her mate returned from their days of exhibiting. He was to continue for another four years and travel far on the Continent, but she died less than a year after the little troupe landed in England, thereby causing her exhibitor much inconvenience and financial loss.

Hadlock must have been fond of her, though he makes no mention of sorrow at her untimely death, to have brought her picture back with him. Evidently it was always treasured by the family, since they took great risk in saving it from a burning house. The woodcut may have been one of others struck off by some local artist to be used on handbills or hung up to attract patrons in the towns where they stopped. But this is all surmise. The only fact I can vouch for is the picture's actual existence.

Samuel Hadlock refers to the pair sometimes as Esquimaux; sometimes as Indians or "Ingens," which would indicate that he billed them as the latter. Indians from North America would undoubtedly have had more popular appeal abroad. The feathered headdress in the picture suggests this, and Hadlock would not have scrupled at accuracy of costume when good English shillings were his object.

At the start it is more than likely that Hadlock had an agent. He mentions a mysterious Mr. Chidingdon in the early pages, one who fell ill in Wales and had to be left behind "whare now person cood understand him for thay spoke all Weltch." Whether Mr. Chidingdon was an agent or merely a chance acquaintance made on shipboard, he soon disappears from the Journal, and Hadlock began his business venture alone. "I proceeded on to the Island of Angelsee," he writes of his first taste of showmanship. "Excibited at Blue Moris and severill other towns on the Island." It was appropriate that he should have chosen another island to open the exhibition. Perhaps he felt more at home on island soil; perhaps shrewd showman's instinct led him there. At all events he had sense enough to begin his enterprise in smaller places where he need not fear competition, and where audiences would be less critical than those in cities and at the famous fairs that were later to bring him such large profits.

From entries farther on in the Journal it would appear that the other exhibits than the human ones were extensive and difficult to transport. Several times he mentions his goods going by van, while he and the Indians traveled in coach or carriage. Some months later on the journey between Bristol and London he mourns the loss of a valuable bale of goods worth a hundred pounds sterling and containing "all the best of the Cuorsities . . . and all of the Indian dresses." There must also have been a booth to be set up even when the exhibiting was done in a hired hall. In Leipzig, a couple of years after, there is mention of a ten-day stop in order to have a booth built "for to Excibit in the Fare." There were beside furs and stuffed seals and birds to be shown, all manner of native weapons—spears, harpoons, and bows and arrows, as well as a collapsible canoe, probably of skin, for the Esquimau man to perform feats of skill and marksmanship on any sheet of water that might come handy.

This was the Esquimau's special act, and only the more important stops warranted this extra display. He seems to have been particularly successful in this on the Continent, where he often performed for kings and queens and members of royal families in palace gardens. But only once in the entire Journal is he referred to directly by name. That is in Bristol where Hadlock notes that "George was taken sick."

They must have been familiar figures in Dublin, where with their exhibitor they spent the five months from January, 1822, till early June. With him they had crossed to Ireland in the King's Steam Packet, and all were soon established in lodgings at the corner of Sackville and Abbey streets. No cheap quarters in a side street for Samuel Hadlock. He liked the good things of this world, and he took them as his right. He hailed from a country that had declared all men to be born free and equal. But it must be confessed that Samuel Hadlock felt himself considerably more than the equal of most men he met. So it was fitting that he should set up on the finest street in Dublin and take the air with the best on St. Stephen's Green.

"A plesant walk indeede on Sunday," he notes in the Journal. Here, a little in the wake of their tall guide in his greatcoat, the Esquimau pair must have excited curious stares from the "many thousen that walk thare of the furst class." One would like to know what they wore and how they looked on those Sunday strolls, and if the little papoose blinked bright eyes from his mother's shoulder at the citizens of Dublin.

Chapter V

For to admire and for to see,
For to behold this world so wide.
—KIPLING.

ALTHOUGH Samuel Hadlock went before the Right Honourable Lord Mayor of Dublin "to gitt permition to excibitt thare," and although his license to do so cost him two pounds and ten shillings, Ireland proved a poor field financially. "Dun little good" is his brief comment on those months in Dublin.

Perhaps his early training in making the best of adverse winds, waiting on tides and accepting all the vagaries of New England weathers, made Hadlock better able than most to cope with the ups and downs of the show business. Perhaps his was simply a large and hopeful nature, that shed present failure as he moved on to a more fortunate next step. So many projects sprang into his head that his feet were hardly set firmly on one venture before his brain was conceiving another. His own

God's Pocket

bottomless well of energy kept him continually stimulated. Like the jugglers at those fairs he was to visit, he must keep all the balls he tossed into the air going at once. Schemes were his juggling balls, and if one fell by the way there were always plenty more up his sleeve. There was not time for regret and brooding. His Journal scarcely ever gives a hint of complaint or disappointment at loss and discomfort in all those four years of wandering. He took the world and his own fortunes as they came, with that largeness of mind and that straight-seeing eye which were the heritage of those earlier seafaring men.

If, with all this resourcefulness and good humor, he was also arrogant and self-willed, it was all part of the pattern of the man. Proud and overbearing as he must have been, he was also one who could take setbacks and rebuffs with good grace. Whether he took in hundreds of pounds or lost them, Samuel Hadlock was one who could see beyond his own pocket and immediate concerns.

So, though Ireland brought him little financial gain, he could readily divert himself with all he saw about him, and he saw plenty of people and places as he went from Dublin to Londonderry. After the clean seaport towns, and the scrupulously neat Cranberry Island houses he had known, it is small wonder that the slack, easy ways of the Irish peasantry should have been a shock to him. His occasional outbursts in the Journal upon the filth and squalor are amusing and spontaneous. "The lower order of the Irish," he writes, "is as meain and Barberish a set of Beinges as ever existed on the face of this erth . . . Thay are so durty as not to wash thair close or houses. You may constentley see them standing in the streetes and the vermin crolling [crawling] over them or see them picking of those Irish tirants out of thar close by 100, so it is most impossible to pass the streetes except catching sum of them." It is easy to guess from the elegant stock, fur collar, and well brushed hair of the London silhouette, that he must have been quite a dandy, and these "Irish Tirants" more than offensive.

"As I was passing threw the cunterey in Ierland," he continues the painful subject, "I saw a sign up for Good Drye Lodgins. I asked a gentleman what thay ment by good drye lodgins. He laft and verey kindly told me that it was Drye Straw. Those lodgings was ondley for poor peple and thay charged ondley one penny per knight and when the onist [honest] loger arois in the morning he was oblige to pull off his close and shake them before he kuld [could] gitt out of the hous as he was over lading [overladen] with vermin.

> A pretty Story indeede
> for a true American to reede"

he winds up in lyrical disgust.

God's Pocket

Poverty of this squalid sort appalled him. Again and again he was moved to mention some instance of it as he traveled from Dublin through Belfast, Drogheda, Limavady, and Coleraine. In one of the smaller towns of County Antrim he observed the flax-growing and various processes in the manufacture of hand-loomed linen, marveling that the laborers should receive only a shilling for their day's work.

"At knight," he notes, "thay return to thare little hutes. Thare supper consists in buter-milke and potatoes which when thay have anythinge for a shift, it is the same over again. The Poore of the Irish due not know how to eate anythinge else but potatoes and buter-milke. To set a peas of good rosted beefe thay wood knot know what it was. Thay wood kall thare next dore nabour to ask and if thay told them that it was beefe & on friaday thay wood run out of the houses if thay ware Cathilickes. . . ." Even in the more prosperous towns, where there were comfortable inns for travelers on the post routes, he continued to marvel at the number of huts and hovels. "The poorest sorte of houses are built of mud and kuvered with straw. The catill and horses lies in the hous with the peple . . . when thare potatoes is boiled thay turn them on the table and all staind round and help themeselves tell the hogues [hogs] komis [comes] and over turnes thare table and spills thare potatoes and the wife says:—Bad luck, will you be out of that now!"

29

God's Pocket

How he must have relished hearing that County Antrim housewife give cry! It is shrill across the yellow pages today, as if the words were scarcely out of her mouth. Hogs and families on such intimate terms about the supper table were certainly not to be encountered on Big Cranberry. No doubt Samuel Hadlock stored this away to regale his neighbors at home, especially the Bulgers and Hamors—both having emigrated from Ireland some years before.

It may have been for their benefit that he set down how many vessels he saw in Belfast Harbor loaded with Irish emigrants for St. John, New Brunswick, and the United States. "Thay lay in provisions annuff to last them one weeke for thare voige," he explains. "Sum of them starve to deth on thare way from this to the United States of Americay. Those that survive curs old Ierland." St. John lies only a couple of hundred miles or so east of Mount Desert, and he must often have seen the pathetic remnants of these emigrant shiploads set ashore, so different from the gay and hopeful groups he now saw putting out of Belfast Harbor, with its lofty green hills "whereon is gentlemen's sumer houses and plesant plantations."

Of all that he saw in Ireland, the Giants' Causeway stirred and excited him most. He stopped at Coleraine, Cold Rane, as he calls it, lying some ten miles distant on a "plesant river that kums to this town." High cliffs and rocky promontories were an old story to Samuel Hadlock, who had sailed under Schooner Head and the sheer sides of Mount Desert Rock, twelve miles at sea. He may have been skeptical as he set off, but since he had heard that the Giants' Causeway was one of the finest natural wonders in the world, he meant to see it for himself. Once arrived there, he stayed to marvel and admire. Gulliver in the land of the Giants could have been no more dwarfed than he before these vast stone columns heaped with geometrical precision. Awe stirred him to the quick as he climbed about, his great sea-boots ringing sharply on the octagonal piles, with the sea breaking far below at their base, and the dim shores of Scotland just visible across twenty miles of Irish Sea.

He was moved to describe at great length this miracle of stone—"the Jients Cosway," is how he spells it. "Thare is a kave runes 200 feete under ground," he writes; "and thare is a cassill [castle] of singular form supost to bin bilt 1400 yeares agoe by the ancient Irish to prevent the Skotch from taking them, for the Skotch and Irish was always at ware with etch other. . . . this Cosway stretches out into Seay as thow it had bin bilt thare by handes. The stones are squair and hued up to a joint and duftailed [dovetailed] together so that you can drive with a carage on top of the Cosway. Thay are piled one on top of another fifteen feete high and of a proper form. At the back of it is lofty hilles." The Giants' Organ especially took his fancy. He reports that "when vued it lookes like the organ of a church." How

31

such strange and regular towers of rock could have been heaped there, and how some of a like formation should also lie across twenty miles of water on the opposite shore of Scotland, piqued his curiosity even as it stirred him. However, just as he begins some personal explanation of this phenomenon, the page ends, and several have been lost from the Journal. Farther on a detached page bears a rough sketch or diagram showing the two coasts and the way the rocks meet under water. Beneath the penciled outlines a careful note has been made: "A complete vue of Ierland taken on the spot and Scotland from the Jintes Cosway in June 15th, 1822. By an old and ancient travelor Seven Hundred yeres agoe."

But whether this is some copy made from an old drawing, or whether the "old ancient travelor" is merely Samuel Hadlock's humorous reference to himself, there is no way of telling.

Chapter VI

I met a gipsy at a Fair . . .—Old rhyme.

Now that hedges and fields and countrysides were green
and flowering again, Samuel Hadlock prepared to make
his hay while the summer sun shone. It was the season
of fairs—cattle fairs, market fairs, horse fairs, and
others in every county and shire of England. Year upon
year they had been held on the same village greens and
in town squares, many of them coming down in direct
succession from the reign of King John and even from
Border times. Here gipsy caravans, peddlers with their
packs, freaks and sword-swallowers galore, clowns and
magicians and tinkers, all flocked to wheedle silver out
of pockets. These farmers and their families who came
to show their wares and to gaze open-mouthed at the
gay tents and booths that sprang up like toadstools in
a single night made stolid, but gullible audiences.

It was a time of exhibitions and exploits. The public,
both of the old world and of the new, was avid for
wonders and curiosities. One has only to run through

33

God's Pocket

files of local New England newspapers of the 1820's to realize that traveling shows and exhibitions of all kinds were as much a part of small-town life as the movies are now. Even in the more or less remote and self-sufficient island community of Nantucket with its strait-laced Quaker families, ventriloquists and sword-swallowers performed, along with exhibitors of pistol sleight-of-hand; apparitions, magnetic and supernatural; dwarfs and freaks, and the feats of a learned elephant. If these flourished in scattered New England villages, the organized fairs across the sea became the Mecca of showmen of that day. There could be no better way to exhibit Genuine Indians and curiosities from the shores of North America, Samuel Hadlock decided, and straightway set about planning his route through the more prosperous ones.

Donnybrook Fair in Ireland seems to have been the first at which he tried his luck, and he reports: "I dun torible wall, concidering I had bin exciberting at Dublin five munthes before." This fair lasted seven days and evidently encouraged Hadlock to try larger ones across the Channel. So he took passage in the steamboat *Mountaineer* and returned to Liverpool. From there the journey continued by canal boat to Preston, where Preston Guild Fair was about to open. He could not have chosen a more important one for his English début, for it was one of the largest and best established. It was held for seven days and happened only once every twenty

34

years. Evidently he had had no idea of its size and popularity or he would have arrived earlier. As it was, all the best places had been secured in advance by others.

"When I goot thare," he writes, "lodinges was 20£. per weeke and I kood not git a room in the town to Excibit in, so I did not make mutch at that time." A hundred dollars for a week's lodgings in any rural place today is no casual sum, and it must have been a small fortune in the 1820's. This single mention of prices and the occasional listing of license fees gives one a new idea of the capital needed for even so small an enterprise as Samuel Hadlock's. Profits must have run high indeed if fair privileges came so dear.

But Preston itself pleased Hadlock. He calls it a "butiful inland town on a high hill." He makes special mention of the fine prospect over the rolling countryside, but of the town's fifty thousand inhabitants he notes that they are "all purtey ritch" with "plenty of Inglish pride." With some amusement he adds, "they can't go out of thare house be what they must have thare carage and 4 livery servantes with them." A far cry to Cranberry Island, where even a bound-out girl was a novel luxury.

Some miles from Preston another fair was to be held at Ormskirk, to which he naturally gravitated, along with other exhibitors. This fair seems to have been the chief event of the year for the whole region, and though the town ordinarily numbered about seven thousand, during the four fair days, its population swelled to ten thousand and more. At such times it was principally given over to the showing of "catill and horse and piges and clothe," the Journal records, "and after thare fares are over the peple has spent all of thare muney so the plase is verey dull and little of knew business duing . . . and thay must goe to work again."

The exhibit from North America no doubt became the subject of much conversation in those small inland towns after fair time was over, and the big, broad-shouldered Yankee and his queer troupe had moved on to fresh pastures and fuller purses—to Wigan and Reading, to Nottingham and Lincoln and Hull.

Competition often ran high. It was no easy matter to get these country people into a booth with as many as a dozen, and sometimes even a score of other near-by attractions. In the neighboring town of Darbey, Hadlock notes that there were thirty-five shows all performing at one time, and England "continuelly sorounded with excerbitions." In spite of this he is able to report that he "dun wall," which must have meant that profits ran to a considerable number of pounds. The equipment and magnificence of some of these other shows amazed him. He was much impressed by traveling bands of clowns and theatrical performers who went about in elaborately decorated, commodious caravans—or "calivanes," as he spells them. These often required eight or ten horses to draw them and contained fine, comfortable rooms in

God's Pocket

the body of the van. There were even some with platforms large enough for the performances to be staged upon them. "The men and wimin perade," he writes, "drest in theatrical aperill [apparel], all spangled and paint themselves. The clounes are drest in a singular form so to tract atention. Thay som dayes take forty or fiftey pound a daye and at nite spend the same."

In spite of these rivals he prospered, and he took good care that no pickpockets made off with his receipts. Apparently organized gangs of these petty thieves were regular attendants at all fairs, doing almost as thriving a business as the showmen. "This is thare hobey," he writes from Nottingham of these light-fingered vagrants, "persuing the same mode of life for thare suport. Som gentlemen drest up respectable watch thare time. When a qurill [quarrel] takes plase and ruse [rush] into the croude and picke pockets, taken thair chans [chance] and robe gentlemen of thar watches or anything thay may have in thair pockets." After this he goes on to recount how the same fellows "shift thair dresses and return to the croude and begin thair roots [routes] tell som of them gitis taken up."

This seems to have been the case often enough and the penalty was a high one. Usually the offender, if convicted, was sent to serve a seven-year term at Botany Bay, from which prison few returned. "Fairs is a little Hell apan Erth," he winds up, "but it is the fashion of

37

this cunterey to permit them so that the farmers can sell thare perduse [produce]."

Samuel Hadlock himself was to have a taste of British authority before he was through with county fairs. But he proved more than a match for the small-town constables of Hull and Lincoln. He had no intention of being sent to Botany Bay or seeing the inside of any jail just when he was beginning to prosper.

Mamie Megunticook was the innocent cause of this trouble, for in one of these fair towns—Gainsborough, perhaps, or Nottingham—she fell ill. There is no mention of her sickness and its tragic end. We shall never know what befell her or if she lies under the alien soil of some English country churchyard. Perhaps she and the little papoose were not even allowed this last privilege. Perhaps there was a secret burial by night at some lonely crossroad with Samuel Hadlock and her Esquimau husband the sole mourners. Perhaps she died alone; perhaps the little papoose died with her. There is no mention of the baby, and if George and Hadlock had been left to tend such a young child, there would undoubtedly have been some reference to this added care. The English climate has never been kind to visitors from other zones. The Indians brought back by Sir Walter Raleigh and other early explorers all succumbed sooner or later to the damp and unaccustomed ways of civilization. Mamie Megunticook, though she had been young and vigorous, was not proof against this, and those months of travel by packet and canal boat and coach were long and arduous. At best, the food was different from Esquimau fare. There were hot noon suns and fogs and driving rains more difficult to contend with than long months of cold and dark spent in some snug, tallow-lit snow-house. Epidemics and fevers flourished in the crowded fair grounds. It was small wonder that she fell easy prey to germs she had never encountered in the far north.

But of his discouragement at this turn of ill luck, Samuel Hadlock gives no hint. He was used to setbacks, and even so serious a one as this did not dismay him. He did not say, "The show must go on," because it simply never occurred to him that it could stop. Death was sad and unfortunate. While the Esquimau woman lived, he spared no money and pains to save her. But once she was dead and buried he must look about for a substitute. He had always had to be resourceful, tricking tides and cross currents, and outwitting head winds and weathers as he now determined to outwit his public.

Casting his eye about him, he immediately hit upon a gipsy woman as the most likely possibility. There were plenty of gipsies on every road to and from fair towns, and silver could readily hire one for almost any purpose. They were of all sorts and sizes and colors, and one was easily found to step into Mamie Megunticook's shoes, or, more accurately, her costume of sealskin and leather. If she wore these well and made an effective

God's Pocket

figurehead, Hadlock decided they could manage. He still had George to speak the native guttural and to entertain with his aquatic exhibitions. But in this he reckoned without taking stock of gipsy temperament.

The first direct reference to this subterfuge in the Journal's pages is in an account of their stay at Hull. Seaport towns were always favorite stopping places with Samuel Hadlock, and here he felt at home along the docks, since Hull sent out "everey yeare twenty sale of shipes to Grenland for whale." No doubt he met with old acquaintances and made new ones among waterfront captains and crews during his ten-day stop there. "Dun Wall," he writes, and adds, "I wass visited by maney a Grenland coptin which had bin maney a voige on that corse. Thay ware verey mutch plesed to behold peple from that cunterey."

But his next step proved less fortunate. A large fair was about to open at Lincoln, so with this for objective he set off with his troupe. All went well at the start, until he records that "the Madistrate found out that one was a Jipesey." She seems to have conducted herself rather well for the first few days of the exhibiting. It was nearly a week before wind of his trick began to get about the fair grounds. The gipsy, although she evidently looked the part, was far less dependable than her predecessor. She may have been indiscreet in hailing some of her cronies, especially when she had had more to drink than was good for her. At all events it was not

40

God's Pocket

long before she gave herself away, and Samuel Hadlock knew he was in for trouble. He must have found her almost more than a match for him and cursed the day he hired her. "The Jipsey that I drest up in sealskin and excibited as an Indian Woomern"—so he refers to her in no flattering terms.

It was not long before her careless talk and rash ways brought things to a pass. Only quick wits and a dash of Yankee spunk saved them all from disaster. It may have been that Hadlock had friends among other exhibitors who gave him warning; or it may have been that in his strolls about the fair grounds he picked up unfavorable comments and complaints. We shall never know how he discovered that he was in immediate danger of arrest. He simply reports that "the Magastrates found out that I was imposing on the Publick. Thay was determined to stop me and send us to prison for the efence commited on the publick."

That was enough for Samuel Hadlock. Remembering the fate of the pickpockets, he dared not risk the chance of being brought to justice. He was canny enough to guess that an exhibitor from the United States would be less leniently dealt with in the matter of heavy fines or even a jail sentence. His exit from the fair was therefore an exceedingly quick one.

"But I goot knues [news] of the same," he writes of the impending arrest with perhaps undue, but pardonable relish, "and sot off that daye at another town and

the town of Granthum
Is a fine inland town great tread Corne
Cos thare in the fattoning line and other.
Comoditiey But in fair time this town
Is very brisk I stopt thare a few Dayes and
went to the Next town whare I stop one
Weke Oure tenitele wall left this town
And past thrune many other towns which
Is too numoraey to mention turned the gipsey
Oup and took both for london kode Nintey
Milldes and Arived at lunden that great
And notid Sittey stopt thare three weekes
And went to the buntersy again gut another
Womenn which ansead my pumpey Better
then the first She being the Same kuffen
And the Same fetchern which prases withou
Dispute She Londeukey her Self Better
then the gipsey   Sunday May the 3th 1823
I note this in pickidilley

God's Pocket

cleaned myself of them and laft at thare under taking. . . . Begun in another town at the same trade. Dun Wall."

He crowed a little too soon, however, for the gipsy woman was not one to change her spots overnight. Farmers might be gullible and less suspicious in the next small towns where they performed, and shillings might mount into pounds, but women were still variable. This particular member of what he called "the frale sect" became an increasing nuisance. He may have been thinking of his trials at the gipsy's hands when later, on a loose page of the Journal, he states with considerable relish that "wiming [women] are deapear [deeper] then the Devill . . . and deserve to be numbered with him." This one certainly had many of his wiles, as her impresario was to discover.

At Grantham she became so unmanageable that even Samuel Hadlock reached the end of his resources and realized there could be no keeping her. "Dun middling wall," he writes, "concidering that I had but wone Indian. The Jipesey wass a Drunken Dissipated Cretour so I kood not depend upon hur. The other logers would tell that she want an Ingin which would git whispered about the town in a fue owers [hours]. So it provented peple of kuming to see them which dun me mutch hurt at aney plase that I went." So without more ado he threw her out and took coach for London, "that great and notid Sitty."

43

God's Pocket

This first stay in London was probably a business trip, for there is little mention of sight-seeing and none whatever of exhibiting. His aim and object was to find another woman for the show. By this time he had learned to be more careful in the selection. It seems to have taken the better part of three weeks to get one that answered all requirements of color, size and exemplary behavior. Where he found her and what she looked like is another matter Samuel Hadlock did not see fit to record. But she was probably a foreigner of some sort, for he was careful to mention her complexion. "Gut another womern," he says, "which ansored my purpes better then the first, she being the same kuller [color] and the same fetchers [features] which pases without Dispute. She conducks hurself better then the Jipsey. . . . I rote this in Pickidilly."

44

Chapter VII

Menagerie to me
My neighbor be——
　　　　　—EMILY DICKINSON.

HE DID not linger long in London. Less populous and busy towns yielded better harvests of good silver pounds, as Samuel Hadlock had already discovered. So, though he evidently put up at one of the best inns and enjoyed the sights of Piccadilly and the Strand, he was off again in a few weeks to continue his round of fairs and rural towns. This time he struck inland, and we find him recording stops at Reading, Cheltenham, and Abingdon. In spite of a spell of bad weather profits were good, and the new member of the troupe gave him little anxiety. It was a novel experience for this island-bred man to go about in these rich inland valleys with their great estates, and the picturesque stone and thatch-roofed cottages of tenant farmers. He found it a pleasant, healthy region, and the cleanliness of such small, agricultural centers particularly appealed to him after the squalor he had met with in some parts of Ireland and at congested fair grounds.

Old buildings everywhere aroused his interest and

45

wonder. One in the town of Abingdon particularly took his fancy, but though he speaks of it as "one of the most finest buildinges of aney inland town," he fails to say if it was guild hall, almshouse, or county seat. What impressed him as much as the building itself was a remarkable apple tree growing beside it. "Thare standes the species of ferbiding [forbidden] frute," he writes. "This apell tree alwayes containes its frute and never drop off. Thay are so hard that know wone [no one] can bite them. Much more mite bin said," he ends with wry amusement at his own evident discomfiture.

At Cheltenham, nine miles farther, he observed more mineral waters and warm springs, which, though less romantic than those of Holywell, nevertheless interested him from a medical standpoint. He found them "warm and of a sulpher taste which will fisick [physic] aney person in fifteen minutes." No doubt he spoke from personal experience in this as in other matters.

Just why Samuel Hadlock decided to walk from that town to Oxford will always be unexplained. It could not have been lack of money, for he had done good business, and lavish spending was one of his weaknesses. Probably he had grown tired of coaches and cramped quarters, and this rolling, midland countryside invited him to stretch his long legs. Stretch them he certainly did in a thirty-mile walk that, according to the Journal, took him all of one pleasant Sunday. There is no mention that George, the Esquimau, accompanied him, so it is likely that he went by post coach with the rest of the outfit. Samuel Hadlock would not have minded going alone. In most of his earlier enterprises he had played a lone hand, and although he was gregarious by nature, he could also be self-sufficient and reflective when concerns of the moment were not too pressing. Then, too, he was possessed of a sort of divine curiosity whether he happened to be watching the flight of a bird in air, or the unfamiliar ways of people in the farms and villages he passed. Even when he mixed most easily with all manner of men—drovers and farmers on the road, peddlers and other travelers in inns and barrooms where he stopped, he was always observant, watching for that deviation from pattern which never failed to stir him.

With all his native hard-headedness and common sense, there was a thoughtful, ruminative turn to his mind. On the rare occasions when this joined forces with the poetic strain in him, there might be sudden and unexpected philosophic outbursts. Wonder crops out in him like a vein of quartz in New England granite. A little book learning is a dangerous thing, or as the down east saying goes, "Too much reading rots the mind." Certainly Samuel Hadlock's mind was free of any such handicap. No secondhand opinions were there to color his own reactions to people and places; to make him self-conscious in expressing what he felt as he went his way through England and the Continent in the 1820's.

God's Pocket

His is the spontaneousness of a child, with the experience of a shrewd man-of-the-world, in the widest sense of that phrase. He never lost this will to seek and question or grew callous to the familiar miracles of tides and seasons. The courses of the sun and moon and the stars in the heavens; the magnetic forces of the earth in its orbit, never became an old story to him. The same problems that absorbed Copernicus and Euclid and Sir Isaac Newton possessed this Island man as surely as if he had been able to spell correctly and find his way about in the intricacies of higher mathematics. He would have felt no inferiority whatsoever in hobnobbing with any of the three, or in giving them his opinions on the state of the universe.

It may well have been on that day's walk between Cheltenham and Oxford that he pondered on things natural and strange, though he was not to set them down in his Journal until another spell of leisure. "A Brief Survey of the Universe" is the somewhat ambitious title he gives to these later observations. It is curious to find them sandwiched casually between a chronological list of important events from the creation of the world, through the Christian era and on up to the death of King George III in 1820, and another long list of English words with their German equivalents. This essay on the universe is less spicy and individual than Samuel Hadlock's more personal comments on people and places, but for all its floweriness and borrowed

God's Pocket

phrases from the Psalms, almanacs, and some forgotten textbook, there is vigor and awe in his explanations of the solar system. When he speaks of the planets, Jupiter, Mars, and Saturn by name, and of the lesser stars in their "annual orbits" one is moved again by the same wonder he was not ashamed to feel and set down. "Thousens of suns multiply without end," is a phrase that King David or John Milton might have been glad to claim.

He speculated, too, upon the possibility of human life on the planets. "From what we know of our own systom," he observes, "it may be reasonabley concluded that all the rest are with equal wisdom contrived, situated and provided with accommodations for Rational inhabitentes."

But he could turn easily from the profound to the practical, and Oxford was to prove a new experience to him. He arrived in a pouring rain at noon of the day following and at once set about taking lodgings and finding a proper place to house the exhibition. "A fine inland town," he calls it. "Fifteen hundred studentz thare, lordes and great gentlemen's sunes [sons] from London . . . most magnificent buildinges." His personal observations of this mellow university town give little hint of scholastic quiet or meditative calm. "Thay are a rude set of fellows," is his comment on the students. "Thay ware all goundes and kapes to distinguish them from the other town peple. Five or six hundred at a time thay make bludey work. Thay have to keepe solgers constentley thare to keepe orders. When the solgers openes [fire] the mob dispurces amedintley to thare quarters. I stopt thare three weekes. Dun torable wall concidering the wether so bad."

Bath came next on their itinerary. It was not the fashionable resort of Beau Nash's day. The luster of the Grand Pump Hotel was not so bright as it had been. But the gentry of England still found it a spa worth visiting, and Hadlock could hardly have failed to hear its praises sung as the peak of elegance and fashion. He may also have heard of the ruins of the Roman baths, though the present extensive excavations of these were not made until fifty years after his visit. Perhaps this is the reason we find no mention of them in his Journal, for with his love of antiquities and his passion for cleanliness such luxurious bathing equipment as the Roman Legion established there would surely have stirred his imagination. It is strange, too, that only one short paragraph is devoted to the city itself.

The only explanation of this is that Bath did not apparently receive the North American Exhibition as cordially as its owner had expected. Although he stayed there three weeks, the terse "Dun nothing" leaves little doubt of his reception. Wealthy visitors to the mineral waters were too sated and sophisticated to bother much with Indians and Arctic curiosities, and Samuel Hadlock, in his turn, had small patience with them. "The quality visit this town for the minerill watters," he writes, making short work of them. "Thay have no other imploy but goe about from one part of the cunterey to the other and spend thare muney with thare families, cariges and servantes. Som of these famlies spend sum hundreds in a day with thare parties. Thay are all ritch peple. Thay dont care for sum thousends to spend in pleshure."

There were no idle rich on Big Cranberry Island, where leisure was at best caught in brief snatches between long voyages or shifts of farming and fishing. Silver was heavy in Samuel Hadlock's strong box, but he had made it himself, by his own wits and energy. We can picture him marveling, with just a shade of contempt, at the men and women of fashion as their carriages rolled by him on the cobbled streets, or as he saw them drifting about the Pump Room in gay groups, absorbed in a world that must have seemed trivial and pointless in contrast to his own. It was the post-Napoleonic period, with military dress uniforms still to the fore. Men wore fitted greatcoats of rich, dark colors. Their stocks were high and set off with bands of fur. Boots glistened, and vests had not been shorn of their splendor. Women had not yet discarded the elaborate poke bonnet and the clinging, high-waisted dresses that the Empress Josephine had favored. We may be sure that Samuel Hadlock missed nothing of all this, for he was far from indifferent to fashion. How could he have helped knowing, being just past thirty and well built ("dark and high-stepping," is how his grandson described him to me), that he cut a fine figure himself in a double-breasted coat of bottle-green or maroon?

After Bath there were other and more profitable stops at Frome and at Bristol, where he found a ship to carry the letters he wrote home telling of his doings in those months that were fast turning into years. It was at Bristol that George, the Esquimau, fell ill, right in the midst of a Spring Fair that had lately opened. We do not know the nature of this illness. Indeed, it is only from the brief mention of his return to health that we know he also suffered from the hazards of show life and the English climate. Another misfortune befell them on the road between Bristol and London, when the valuable bale of goods was stolen from the van. Either by chance or by intent, the thieves happened to make off with the one containing all the best of the Arctic curiosities. These were unreplaceable, and there was nothing for Hadlock to do but make shift without them as best he could.

So it was London again. Once more he faced delays until George recovered and the show could be put in shape to reopen. I am convinced that it was during this enforced spell of leisure that he sat for his silhouette likeness; and it was characteristic that he should have gone to one of the most noted artists in scissors and paper. The first thirty years of the nineteenth century marked the peak of popularity for this form of portrait. All over England, the Continent, and America, traveling artists of real or indifferent talent snipped the shadowed profiles of whole families, singly or in groups. The boldness and beauty of this particular silhouette cut from dark red paper and touched with gilt in fine, free brush strokes to suggest the hair and fur, would mark it as the work of a more than usually skillful artist, even if one could not trace the signature "Foster 1824" under the bust.

Foster seems to have been one of the best scissor and brush artists of his time, though he is not so well known as Edouart, the Frenchman, who visited the United States ten years later and cut likenesses of important Americans from Boston to New Orleans. "Profilist from London," so Edward Ward Foster described himself in an advertisement in a Derby newspaper in 1811, but he was apparently careless about signing his portraits. That Hadlock should have made sure that the artist signed his, is another proof of his Yankee hard-headedness. Having made up his mind to pay for a silhouette by the most fashionable artist in London, he saw to it that the authentic stamp was not forgotten. It must have tickled his pride to know that his profile was cut from the same paper as those of the nobility who patronized Foster's studio. I have seen a reproduction of a Foster likeness of the Countess of Blessington, cut at about the same time. It hangs in Knole Castle, but it might be a companion piece to the one packed away in the old trunk on Cranberry Island.

But for all such pleasant diversions, the London venture did not prove successful. Competition ran high there at all times, and it was particularly unfortunate that a rival exhibit of Laplanders and "the Botokado Indian," whoever he may have been, had already been shown there. These had stolen his thunder, as Samuel Hadlock was not slow to discover. So once more he turned his back on the "great and notid Sittey."

It is probable that he made a second trip to Dublin and Londonderry at this time, for there are two sets of entries on both these places. But this section of the Journal has been resewn, and often pages are missing or out of place, which makes following his route difficult. Then, too, Samuel Hadlock was not always accurate, even when he took the trouble to mention dates. But, dates or no dates, he manages to set down a very vivid, first-hand account of some races he witnessed. These seem to have been held near Londonderry and to have attracted a tremendous following. "Peple kums from all partes of Ingland," he notes with amazement, "to these rases that havens [happens] wons a yeare."

Horse-racing could hardly have been a familiar sport to him in a country of thickly wooded shores and rough roads. The horses he had seen were probably bred for use rather than speed, and this may well have been his first sight of a race track. From his account the events appear to have lasted for more than one day, and he was there from start to finish. It was a spectacle which must have delighted his heart. We can guess how he gave himself to the occasion, mingling with the throngs of holiday spectators; elbowing his way to the front when the horses were led out on view; listening to the shrill urgings of men in the betting stands; watching with his keen, seafaring eyes as he stood head and shoulders above the crowd at the finish line.

"The furst day," he writes, "twenty rais horses of the finest blud run for one hundred ginnes [guineas] which was won by the finest hors." Next day the stake was for ten times that sum, and it seems to have been carried off by the same horse. This may or may not have been lucky for Samuel Hadlock, for if he put his money up on any entry, he makes no mention of it. It is scarcely credible that, with his love of chance and his easy enthusiasms, he could have resisted such a temptation. But it is also extremely unlikely that he could have kept mention of any winnings out of the Journal.

The horses were apparently given a rest on the third and last sporting day, and human sprinters took their places. These contestants were evidently all champions, and he tells how they competed for the gold cup offered by the Corporation, with the Duke of Sussex and other members of the nobility looking on. The skill of these athletes was a revelation to him, just as the sight of fine horse-flesh on the race track had been. "The last day," he writes, "two men run for three hundred guines. . . . Thay strip off all but a pair of drows [drawers] . . . and run two mildes in fifteen minites." For this final event the stake was three hundred guineas, and of the two rivals for it, the man from Lancaster came in ahead. But he adds that a gentleman gave twenty guineas to "the wone that was beete," an act of generosity which impressed him greatly.

And so we come to the last entry in his British notebook, set down in Hull in the early summer of 1824: "I took passage in the Brig Capt. Skarborough for Hamburg in Jerminey on the continent to try my fortune thair."

56

Chapter VIII

There is nothing which has yet been contrived by man, by which so much happiness is produced as by a good tavern or inn.
—Dr. Johnson.

It was no less significant a day than July Fourth when Samuel Hadlock set foot on the Continent. Hamburg was the port, and the year 1824, more than two years since he had left the country which was uppermost in his thoughts as the *Captain Scarborough* picked its course up the river Elbe from Cuxhaven at the mouth. The morning was fine and blue and the water alive with shipping. Even the harbor of Liverpool had not been so cluttered with "vessills from all partes of the world." The sun was bright on canvas, new and weather-worn, and on all the steep gabled houses that time, and a fire some twenty years later, were to level.

Watching it all, and thinking of the new enterprises ahead, he was suddenly taken with an attack of patriotism, of the sort that other travelers have felt at the threshold of a strange country. The American Revolution was still close to him. His father and men of that generation had fought and lived through it. Samuel Hadlock, Jr., had been twenty when the War of 1812 broke out, and though he took no very active part in it, "freedom" and "liberty" were not yet overworked words in text-books and Independence Day addresses. They meant the present and future to him as well as the past, and so he writes of them. "I arrived on that glorious day coled the forth of Julye," he notes. "Evereay true sitison of Columbias hapey land shood bair in mind and remember on that day she shook off the yoke of a tiranikall government and fread hurself of maney Imbarissments that iss imposed on hur mother cuntrey. When I contemplate on the Imposition that the subjecks of the old cuntrey labors under I have the gratior hart to astoll that land cold America and hur free suns that Reside thair and who no not the want of liberty."

This lofty mood was not, however, long sustained, and we find him turning to the more practical needs of himself and his troupe. Probably because he was ignorant of even the most rudimentary German, he hired an agent. This man, who never appears by name in the Journal, must have made the most of their two months' association. He immediately arranged for the exhibition to open in his own residence, the Simon Mansion hotel, no doubt reaping a neat commission from the

58

owners, since the monthly rent was two hundred dollars. Again the cryptic "not dun much" leaves us wondering whether the agent shirked his responsibilities, or if Hamburg, used as it must have been to strange cargoes and outlandish visitors from all parts of the globe, was indifferent to the novelty of North American Indians. But the lack of patronage did not seem to worry their exhibitor, who found plenty of diversions, especially of an evening in this port that catered wholeheartedly to the fancy of sailors ashore from long voyages.

Samuel Hadlock was nobody's fool. He had more than his share of animal spirits, and he was not one to deny the appetites of the flesh. But for all that, he hailed from a narrow community in the still more or less Puritanical-minded New England. Prostitution, especially in thriving seaports, must have been an old story to him, but the free and easy acceptance of it, not only by the authorities, but by the most eminently respectable of the townspeople, was something he had never expected to encounter. His amazement grew as he made his nightly visits to the more notorious bars and saloons, and his entries are a curious mixture of Yankee disapproval at the mixed company, and masculine admiration of the "ladies of pleshier" all about him. How much he knew of them intimately, the Journal gives no hint, but that no smallest detail of their ways and wiles escaped him, is plain from these

God's Pocket

two pages. That they managed to survive pruning later on by his wife and daughter, is nothing short of a miracle. Only one word has been erased from the whole spicy account, and in no other part of the complete record is one so aware of Samuel Hadlock the man. Though his upbringing cautioned disapproval, he relished his first taste of continental liberty. He would not let himself condone the system that was against all his own and his neighbors' moral standards; but while he disapproved, he went from one bar to another, with all the shrewd appreciation of the man of the world which he had unconsciously become. He relaxed in the warm and amorous atmosphere of these "gay sites" as he tactfully calls them, and his pleasure must have been heightened by his amused speculations on what the residents of Big Cranberry would have said about his being there.

One of these luxurious places, with an undecipherable name, moved him to a detailed description. "On Sunday Evnings" he notes that it was particularly popular, "a Fashneable plais for most all sortes of peple, gentull and simpill, hors and roges [whores and rogues]. The Dans begines at dark," he goes on, "and is kep up tell one o'clock. I have counted one hundred hors in the Saloon at one time, drest like queans, or rather like venesies [Venuses]. Allso Gentlemen with thair famlies resort this interesting plais, if we may so coll it."

Apparently the sight of respectable families mingling

God's Pocket

so freely in what he had heretofore considered as a different world, came as a shock. But he accepted the custom of the country with easy tolerance, and indeed adapted himself quickly, only feeling called upon to throw in an occasional derogatory phrase to remind himself of his earlier notions of propriety.

With his usual curiosity he inquired into the system. He mentions the number of girls kept for sailors in the different places he visited—twenty-four in one, twenty in another, and so on. "These girls," he records, "have lisens from the polese and pay a taxe for thair fun. Thare are 8 more salones in the town, of respectibilitey as thay coll them." One of these, known as Hamburg Bar, seems to have been especially popular on Sunday. Of this he reports that "the ladies of pleshier resort . . . in the daytime to take coffey or teay and dans the hole day Sunday . . . The ladies when you enter the room," he continues with keen appreciation, "wone wood supose that he wass amungst ladies of the furst class as thay do not drink like the Inglish wimin. Nor have thay so maney bad qualities except with thair . . ." Evidently his language was too frank, for an eraser has been at work, and we shall never know the exact nature of the ladies' offense.

The air of dignity with which these places were conducted also impressed him greatly. "Thay due it," he reports a little farther on in the Hamburg notes, "in a Desent manner in a room provided for that purpurs, whare no wone disturbes them tell fertig [fatigue] deprives them of thair pleshure. Then"—here he cannot quite suppress a Cranberry Island comment—"thay return back like Progale son [Prodigal son] and are hartley recived by thair companions." He must have witnessed many such scenes, and though he could not have understood a dozen German words at the time, he nevertheless felt no hesitance in reporting their probable conversation. Nothing in the whole Journal gives such a glimpse into the half naïve, half sophisticated mind of Samuel Hadlock as the following bit of imaginary dialogue between these girls. Nothing shows his own native brand of humor or his human insight so well.

"We hope that you have Injoid yourselves?"

"O yes, verey wall, I will assure you."

"Wall, I am verey hapey to hear it."

"Heave you not met with a companion yet?"

"No, no, I expect that my old Bo will kum bym by. But I wont wate mutch longer if he dont kum I will gitt som other soon. But I head drother [had rather] heave him. He plesed me so wall the last time I will wate little longer."

So much for the "ladies of pleshier."

62

Chapter IX

"O. I perceive after all so many uttering Tongues."
—WALT WHITMAN.

THE Europe in which Samuel Hadlock found himself was only just beginning to recover from the Napoleonic Wars. It was barely nine years since the smoke of Waterloo had cleared. Napoleon was dead in St. Helena, but his ghost still walked in the Austrian and German cities, where Hadlock was to see with his own eyes relics of the bombardment, and to count as many as two thousand balls in the walls of a single house in one Prussian town. "Hott Shott" is his vivid comment on the burning of one city, and "Boney fott a hevey Batill here" is another phrase that occurs more than once in the Journal. Never once does he refer to the Little Corporal by his full name. He is always Boney, a familiar nickname which persisted among sailors and seafaring men longer than with those ashore. This was probably due to the popular sea chantey about him, of which there are many versions in existence, and which Hadlock no doubt had often sung.

63

God's Pocket

Boney was a warrior. Away-ay—yah!
A warrior and a tarriar, John Franswor.

Boney fought the Roo-shi-ans,
Boney fought the Proo-shi-ans.

Moscow was a-blazing,
And Boney was a-raging.

Boney went to Elbow,
Boney he came back again.

Boney went to Waterloo,
There he got his overthrow.

Boney broke his heart and died
Away in St. Helena.

Drive her captain, drive her.
We're off to Baltimore . . .

These are only a few of the verses, and indeed such an endearing and familiar figure did the sailors make of him that one is hardly surprised to find him crossing the Rocky Mountains in one version!

With his flair for courage and romance, Hadlock could hardly have failed to be stirred by the Napoleonic legend. Leipzig held many souvenirs of the great battle fought there with the Allied Armies pressing the French across the River Elster. He was moved to write a detailed account of the bungling mistake which caused such terrific loss and of Bonaparte's miraculous escape. "Boney lost his Battle and returned home to Frans," he writes. "He was so closely persued that he wass oblige to Retreat through a smoll artchway with his hors. I have often bin through the same plais," he adds with distinct personal relish. "The Enemey wass firing at him within an hundred yardes. At the same time prins lepalow [Prince Leopold] leaped his hors in the stream in order to make his ascape with Boney, but the hors broke his lague and wass dround. After that Boney crost the Brig." He goes on to tell of the Emperor's order to blow up the bridge, supposing that his army was over, and of how this mistake and the seven days' siege that followed cost him about a hundred thousand men. There is nothing especially remarkable in this somewhat garbled account, but it shows how vividly the spell of the Emperor persisted into this post-war period.

Although Samuel Hadlock must have supposed that in going to Germany he was entering a united kingdom, he soon found that it was instead a group of some thirty-nine small and independent states. During the Napoleonic Wars the Holy Roman Empire had been completely disorganized, and the Congress of Vienna in 1815 had sanctioned this State system. Besides the greater principalities of Austria and Prussia, he was to know others—Bavaria, Saxony, Hanover, Württemberg, Brunswick, and Baden—each a complete and separate small world, differing from its neighbors, not only in government, but often even in the language spoken. Although the ruling princes had promised free constitutions to their people as a concession to the spirit of the times, few of them lived up to their word, and in the years that Hadlock spent there he found these independent sovereigns for the most part thorough absolutists in principle and practice. Indeed, he was to see them at home in their palaces; to hobnob familiarly with more than one.

Samuel Hadlock gave himself whole-heartedly to the Continent, as he had not done to England. His spirits rose, and he expanded in the cheerful, less constrained atmosphere of these tidy, small kingdoms. Despite the handicap of language he and the German-speaking people seem to have been temperamentally congenial—a fortunate thing for Hadlock as it later turned out. Even from a casual glance at this second book of his travels the change in him is noticeable. The copy book itself is thicker, with fuller and more personal entries. The handwriting has a swifter pace, and even the spelling has improved. For this last change practice, and his efforts to get a working knowledge of German are probably responsible, for the long lists of German words with their English equivalents must have been copied from dictionaries or taken down by word of mouth from his agent. At all events Germany suited him, and we find him extolling the pleasant, well kept countryside on one of the early pages.

God's Pocket

"This Cuntrey," he writes of an inland part, "is so levill that with your Ies you may look [far?]. Tis like looking to sea in a calm Day, it goes off so reglur." The carefully tended acres of vegetables moved him to admiring comment, and the whole fertile region was a revelation to him after the rocky, hard-won Island farms of his boyhood. "The prospeck," he goes on, "is mutch better then in Ingland. Living is not half so dear as in Ingland or Ireland. Lise [lice] is not so plenty as in padies land." The memory of those "Irish Tirants" still rankles, and he cannot resist the following sly dig. "Thair," he adds, recalling his Irish travels, "thay dont want for meat. If nothing els thay nock down a fine, fat, shining lous and then that will suplye a hole famley for sometime!" The exclamation point is mine, since Samuel Hadlock was as free of punctuation marks as a frog of feathers.

As the month of August, 1824, drew to a close, and Hamburg for all its diversions had not proved a lucrative venture, Hadlock began to plan his next move. It was quite natural that this should have been to Leipzig, for the famous Michaelmas Fair held yearly there in September since the twelfth century. Originally there had been three great fairs there each year—at New Year's, at Easter, and at Michaelmas time. The New Year fair has been abandoned, but the September one which Samuel Hadlock attended has continued an important event, to which merchants and tourists still flock.

God's Pocket

Only last fall I read a newspaper account of the preparations being made for its opening and of the attempt to curtail the activities of Jewish merchants. This, in the year 1933, makes Hadlock's description of the Jews he saw there all the more significant.

"I left this town [Hamburg]," he notes, "on the seventh of September for Lipsick [Leipzig] 200 mildes in the cuntrey to one of the largest fairs in the world." How he traveled there he does not bother to note. Even with strong horses and good roads the journey appears to have taken the better part of nine days; but, though he passed through many towns and some cities, he makes but brief mention of them. Lüneburg on the Elbe interested him chiefly because of its English affiliation, being governed by the Duke of Cambridge.

At the border near Leipzig—or Lipsick, as he persistently calls it—there was official business to be gone through. His little troupe and all his curiosities had to be passed upon by the authorities, and he carefully notes: "I ware oblige to onlode my goodes and have them over hold [overhauled] and to pay duties for the same and then alowd to pass after shooing our passportes." One cannot help wishing that these passports had been preserved along with the Journal and the silhouette, for they would shed light on the Esquimau, George, and give some idea as to the substitute he found for Mamie Megunticook. But they have gone the way of all such, and we shall never know whether

68

God's Pocket

an English gipsy or some other dark-skinned woman completed the little company. There must have been one other besides George, for in later entries it is usually the Indians, not the Indian, that he mentions.

"I arived at Lipsick," the Journal records, "on the 16th of September. Stopt thair tell the 26th and in this time haid a booth built for to Excibit in." Evidently this was all preliminary to the opening of the Fair, for he goes on to say that that lasted for three weeks. "My reseates [receipts]," he adds with satisfaction, "ware $1500. and on Sunday in the afternoon I put the Indian on the watter at . . . for the last time in this town whare I took $600. in 2 owers [hours]. The croudes of spectaters ware great and mutch plesed to behold a native from the arctic regions Exploy [exploit] his boat with such admirable dexteritey and kill his game so wall as he did."

This, and a later reference in Austria, are the only clues we can find to George's actual maneuvers. Apparently his marksmanship as he cavorted in his canoe was nothing short of a sleight-of-hand performance, and only when the crowds warranted such an extra display did his exhibitor allow the water spectacle.

Some notion of the vast attendance at the Fair may be gathered from Hadlock's own statement that, while the town normally contained about sixty thousand inhabitants, during this time it increased to some one hundred and sixty thousand. To have a hundred thousand

69

visitors in three weeks must have taxed it to its limits, but all seems to have been conducted admirably. If there were gangs of pickpockets and rogues, there is no mention of them in the Journal. What aroused Samuel Hadlock's interest and moved him to vivid description were the representatives of hitherto unknown parts of the world,—Southern and Central Europe, and even Turkey and Asia. "The turkes of all men are the worst looking," he comments without reservation. It was his first sight of the Slavic type, and of the Orthodox Jew, and both were repugnant to his preconceived ideas of good looks. He finds the "Poland Jues higeous looking with thair long beardes which comes down to thair waist bands. . . ." But "the Greakes are fine looking men," with features more to his fancy. "The turkes and jues and greakes," he observed, "dress nerleay alike. Those people come to this town with carts ladend with gold to purchious goodes at this fair. Som of them come som thousens of mildes."

There is a ring of the Arabian Nights to that casually set down phrase "carts ladend with gold." It might belong to a thousand, rather than a bare hundred, years ago. Leipzig Fair today is housed in a building somewhat like the Grand Central Palace in New York. Its exhibits are noted for their examples of the modern trend in art, in industry and in book printing, since Leipzig has become the center of the German book trade. Probably if Samuel Hadlock could revisit it today the Orthodox Jews with their long beards would seem the only familiar link with the Fair that he knew in September, 1824.

Chapter X

I have immortal longings in me.—SHAKESPEARE.

ALTHOUGH it is difficult to follow Samuel Hadlock's actual progress about Germany after he left Leipzig Fair, the Journal gives us a fairly accurate idea of the state of his mind at this time. Later resewing of the pages has made it hard to guess what cities were privileged to see the Exhibition from North America, but that he was making for "Barlien" is apparent.

"This is the Capitall of Prushieay," he writes of Berlin, "and the Residens of King fredrick William." This palace seems to have disappointed his expectations, for he dismisses it briefly as "a smoll, old fashion Building." The Crown Prince's palace, however, pleased him better, and on the city itself and its impressive quarters for soldiers he waxed eloquent. "The publick buldens of this town equills aney that I ever saw. The Capitall covers fore akers of land and is most magnifness. . . . Oposit of this [the King's palace] is a large gard hous whare the Solgers Reside. Thare are about twelve more

72

God's Pocket

Capitall Buildginges in this cittey, som older then merthuslem [Methuselah], built in the old stile with more gothick windows which gives them a singlar aperans to the Buldinges of this day."

The fortified walls and the soldiers on guard there impressed him no less than the double life-sized statues he met at every turn. Over one entrance he makes special note of "fling [flying] horses cast in brass." He is amazed that some of these enormous statues should have been carried to France by Bonaparte and later brought back to their old places "with mutch expens." It is rather disappointing not to find him expatiating upon the beauties of Unter den Linden and the elaborately planned miles of Tiergarten stretching out in the direction of Charlottenburg, that suburb which he was to know so intimately a few months later. But though he remarks that the city is finely laid out, he also notes that the streets are dirty as well as broad. "The streates are pavid with round stone," he writes, "so that is hard travilling over them, if too often it will Caus your feat to be sore."

He is more enthusiastic over one part of the "Prominard" where the central blocks have been "polished so that you can see your fais as wall allmost as in a looking glass," and about more "figures of Brass Butifuley Executed. I think it the finist peas of workmenship that I ever saw," he adds, "and I count myself no fool of a judge."

It is from this last simple statement that he launches into a three-page speculation on the works of nature versus the works of man. Once again the poet and philosopher in him got the upper hand of the practical State of Maine showman. The old longing to know and fathom his own particular universe came upon him again, only the more insistent because of what he had seen and experienced in the last two years of travel. To have stepped at thirty, in the vigor of self-assured young manhood, from a remote pocket of the new world into the age-mellowed cities of an older civilization, must have stimulated a far less imaginative man than Samuel Hadlock. In the little world of Cranberry Island, the present and the future had been his chief concerns. The past, for himself and his contemporaries, was at most only a generation and half behind them. Barely a hundred years of living had left its mark on the land they knew. No wonder then that he quickened to a romantic past, whose records he saw all about him in stone and bronze, in canvas and marble. No wonder that he must also link them with the timeless forces of nature which he had learned to recognize and accept, without ever losing his awe of their workings.

"In vuing the workes of nature and man," he begins, "I scars no which to give the gratest prais to. The work of man we can look on and see hough it is Dun. The work of Nature is hid from our vew. Tharefore we are not able to Judge of Hur workes as that of man. Thare-

74

fore we are led to believe that it is cosed by the all wise being which Bigens and finishes his work in Seckrit, nor requires no aprintes nor the handey work of man to help him out with it."

Settled there in his Berlin lodgings, with all the human beings about him talking to one another in an unintelligible tongue, it is not surprising that Hadlock should have found outlet in the Journal. Also it is not strange that by the same token he should leave the abstract rhetoric of his beginning, to put his observations on paper as if he were addressing an imaginary listener.

"Prehapes," he goes on, "that you will think my obersevations quite heroness [erroneous], but when those Ies of thine have sean what I have sean with mine your obersevations wood combind with mine. Then you wood desern this world in another lite. You sopose that you have sean as mutch with thoes Deprived Ies of thine as I have Sean with mine, but let me tell you that you are mistaknd. Allthough myne have sunk so far in my head . . . thay are still able to Disern Diffrent thinges then thine."

There was no inferiority complex in Samuel Hadlock's make-up. Such colossal egotism as his almost suggests the fanatic. But it seems too good-natured and naïve for that. It is, I think, rather a cropping up of the arrogant, self-willed child in the man—the child who is so certain that the Universe has been fashioned to revolve about him. With all his largeness of mind

75

and heart, with his shrewdness and tolerance in his dealings with others, he always knew he was a little better than other men. Or perhaps he was only more frank in admitting the natural superiority most of us are born feeling, but which bitter experience teaches us to hide.

"When I stand and cast my frale Ies around and Behold the Diffrent multitudes of people that I behold, and when I turn and Behold your Shores," he continues, evidently turning his attention now to the inhabitants of Europe and the British Isles, "that is diprived [here he evidently means 'comprised'] of thous multitudes of Diffrent Sex [sects] what can I say besides? When you meat a person you now him and pass the time of day with him, but wass I to due that I shood want ten thousen of tunges and more wisdom then Solomon wass indowed with."

This is the only hint we can find in the whole Journal that Samuel Hadlock was conscious of the barriers of language. Not to be able to "pass the time of day," not to know what men and women were saying as they brushed by him going about their separate ways, was an altogether new experience to this Island man. All who have ever traveled alone in a foreign land know what he felt, whether they have expressed it or not. So, thrown back upon his own resources, he let his pen and thoughts ramble on.

"This Subjeck," the diversity of language, he continues, "will be too long for me to persue, therefore I will close it in Season for fear of ofending the Reador and then he will sopose that he noes as mutch as the Ritor. Tharefore I will not Deprive him of his thotes and he may Maintain his one opinon and think him-Self as wise as the rest of his frendes and Jestified in soduing for a mans vigor often Diprives him of maney thinges that he mite no."

Sudden flashes of insight like this one upon a man's vigor coming between him and wisdom are like sparks struck from flint by one of his own hob-nailed boots. Out of the cluttered and often repetitious jumble of words, a single such phrase will startle with the ring of pure truth and self-perception, in direct odds to the childish conceit and cocksureness of the man who counted himself no fool of a judge on any subject under heaven.

On the very next page appears an extraordinary table of dates and events, with the following paragraph of explanation. "I will Begn a Subijick concerning the Biginning of the World which you will scars Credit, but let me tell you that it is through [true], as I am noing to the hole afair. So dough not dispute the Subjick that I am about to Rite concerning everey King an battill that has bin fought sens fore thousen and fore yeares Before the Birth of Crist, and Everey Mericall that took plais Before Crist's time and Even after up to this date."

God's Pocket

With infinite pains and a fine pen he has copied, evidently from some Almanack of the period, four pages of dates and happenings. Appropriately enough, the first item listed is the Creation of the World in 4004 B.C. From that, through the building of the Tower of Babel; the Israelites in Egypt; the birth of Moses and other biblical events; the siege of Troy; the destruction of Carthage, and Caesar's first expedition to Britain, and other campaigns, it proceeds through the Crusades, into Elizabethan times and on up to the death of George III in 1820. Next comes the even more ambitious discourse, eight pages long, with its all-embracing title: "A Brief Survey of the Universe." This, as I mentioned earlier on the occasion of his walk between Cheltenham and Oxford, must have been derived, in part at least, from some almanac, the same perhaps that furnished him with the list of world events. It is not in itself a remarkable document, but as an indication of the way he spent this brief spell of leisure, and of the range of his speculations, it is significant.

So highly personal a curiosity for things natural and strange is rare in literature. Most often one finds it expressed in poetry. I can never read this section of the Journal without remembering certain lines by a Scotchman of the seventeenth century, whose questionings, though they were expressed lyrically, were of the same stuff that moved Samuel Hadlock to seek and wonder.

78

God's Pocket

To know this world's centre,
Height, depth, breadth and length,
Fain would I adventure
To search the hid attractions
Of magnetic actions
And adamantine strength.
Fain would I know, if in some lofty mountain,
Where the moon sojourns, if there be tree or fountain;
If there be beasts of prey, or yet be fields to hunt in—
  Hello, my fancy, whither wilt thou go?

And then, with no transition whatsoever, Hadlock washes his hands of the universe, and turns all his attention to acquiring enough German to go about his business. With a grand flourish of his pen, he seems to be saying, "And that, my friends, is that!" From now on for half a dozen pages, his mind is set upon nouns and verbs, and such useful phrases as: "Give me a pinch of snuff?" "What is the ower?" "Whither shall I goe?"

Chapter XI

Was ever woman in this humour woo'd?
Was ever woman in this humour won?
—SHAKESPEARE.

THEN suddenly on a winter morning—it may have been December, 1824, or early January, 1825—the whole course of Samuel Hadlock's life was changed. A romantic love, so consuming and torrential that it defied even his usually undismayed pen, took him like a Bay of Fundy tide. He went down before it complete, without a protest. He gave himself entire, as only the few great lovers of the world have been able to do.

Whenever I think of this incredible chapter of his life, I remember the sudden vehemence of spring in northern Maine, and I know how it was with him on that morning in Charlottenburg. I know how the ice breaks with dull thunder; how the barriers go down in a single night; how arbutus and violets spring from melting snows, and a green, fiercer than flame, runs over brown pastures and ledges. No soft, slowly unfolding southern spring ever was so charged with the enduring passions of earth. No sap quickened by the

80

God's Pocket

first hot April sun ever mounted more swift and strong in a tree than the blood in Samuel Hadlock's pulses at that chance encounter.

They must have talked of it often afterwards, rehearsing, with the tireless wonder of lovers, the narrow margin by which circumstance might have tricked them of each other. If he had gone east instead of west; if she had not been left at home; if he had sent some one else to procure the permit for him, how different the rest of their two lives must have been! Even now, after a hundred years, I must marvel, too, though what I know of their love story is brief and brittle, hardly more than the skeleton of a leaf pressed between the pages of an old book.

In the whole Journal there is but one reference to his marriage. There may have been others, removed long afterwards by the Prussian Lady's own hands because they were too poignant reminders of first love in a distant gable-roofed house. It may have been that Samuel Hadlock, usually so candid of expression, turned suddenly secretive in sharing these emotions, which might be less personal and private if set down in writing. If love letters passed between them, as it is more than likely they did during the next six months, none have been preserved.

So there is nothing left for me but to tell the love story as best I can, piecing it together from the account I heard so often from his grandson. Once I might have

81

been tempted to embroider the scanty details. But now I know they must stand for themselves since I have no part in the story.

It was a winter morning when Samuel Hadlock, with the Esquimau at his heels, set off for Charlottenburg. He had decided that this suburb would be a better place for the exhibition than Berlin. The air was so keen and frosty that he had put on his great fur coat (of bearskin, if I remember rightly). It made him look even bigger and taller than he was—a dark, high-stepping man.

Before he could set up the exhibition in any town he must seek out the magistrate and obtain a license at the regular price. This he lost no time in doing. It was to the house of one Ludwig Russ that he was sent to get this permit. Russ, though not a man of high birth, had risen to an important position in the Royal Brass Foundry of Charlottenburg. Even in the 1820's the suburb had become a great industrial center. Its iron and brass foundries were famous and lived up to their names, being directly under the patronage of Frederick William III of Prussia. Herr Russ held a responsible post there and had become wealthy and influential in the affairs of the town. His house must have been imposing, with more than its share of the comforts and luxuries of that time. He had servants and a position to maintain, and his station was only a step below the nobility and lesser royalty, whom he could meet on an equal footing. He had, besides this, a young and lovely daughter.

Dorethea Albertina Wilhelmina Celeste Russ was only a few months past twenty on that winter morning when Samuel Hadlock came, as he had been directed, to her father's house. Ludwig Russ was not at home, and whether by mere chance or because she was in the habit of meeting visitors in her father's absence, she received the tall fur-coated stranger. Hers was a fair, diminutive beauty,—the very blond embodiment of Dresden China charms, and Samuel Hadlock was helpless before her.

She could not speak a word of English, and his few halting German phrases were no use to him now: "A pinch of snuff, if you please," "Kindly direct me to an Inn," and "My horses are in need of shoeing." What good have such as these ever been to a man in love?

It has become the fashion to smile a superior smile at mention of love at first sight. But Samuel Hadlock was born with an eye for wonders, and a heart for the event. He knew the signal, and plunged headlong and confident into this new adventure.

"Who ever loved that loved not at first sight?" Christopher Marlowe cried, out of an earlier time, and Samuel Hadlock would have been the last to contradict him.

Telling me of it a hundred years after, his grandson

never varied his brief recital of this scene by a single word.

"They looked at each other," he would say, "and they knowed."

Chapter XII

You know, my Friends, with what a brave Carouse
I made a Second Marriage in my house.
　　　　—THE RUBÁIYÁT OF OMAR KHAYYÁM.

HE MUST have known, as soon as he knew anything besides the emotions that Dorethea Albertina Wilhelmina Celeste had stirred in him, that this would be no ordinary courtship. The story goes that within the hour he was off seeking an interpreter to present his suit. No grass grew under Samuel Hadlock's feet, and before the day was over he had made a formal proposal of marriage to Ludwig Russ for his daughter.

She may well have been betrothed already at that time. But, even if she were still free, her parents must have had far different plans for her future. I have never heard mention of her mother, but I know that her father opposed the match vigorously. Such whirlwind wooing had never even been conceived of in his well-

85

ordered, conventional world. This daughter, who I think may have been an only child, was certainly the proverbial apple of his eye. She was young and delicately bred, and he had given her every advantage and luxury in his power. He had no intention of letting her go away to the wilds of America. It was inconceivable that in a single morning's absence from home this madness should have come upon her.

He could not deny the attraction of the tall showman from North America, with his fine figure of a man and his proud, impetuous ways. It was not surprising, though extremely unfortunate, that his daughter should have fallen under the spell of his magnetism. As a visitor from across the Atlantic, Ludwig Russ would have welcomed Hadlock to his home; he would not even have resented the free airs he gave himself, as if there were no such thing as class distinctions and barriers of birth to curb personal ambition, but as the self-assured suitor of Dorethea Albertina Wilhelmina Celeste—that was another matter. It was altogether difficult and disturbing. The American's persistence and vitality were past his powers of belief. It made no difference how many times the interpreter conveyed a firm and flat refusal; in another day he was back with his fantastic offer. Even the interpreter had lost all sense of reason. He was actually on this man's side. He had the effrontery to advise in favor of the match. This man Hadlock, he explained, was no ordinary peddler of freaks. He was a capitalist from the new world with plenty of money in his strong box. With the extraordinary ways of these Americans he had not even inquired about the dowry Ludwig Russ might be expected to give his daughter. He was not asking for a penny of her father's money.

This fact could not have failed to impress Russ. He was a hard-headed business man, and like most European fathers he had counted on a future son-in-law who would take a handsome money settlement for granted along with the betrothal. Such utter disregard of personal profit as this was disarming, though quixotic. It was an opening wedge in parental disapproval, and Samuel Hadlock made the most of it.

He and Dorethea Albertina were managing their strange courtship with remarkable ease, considering the gulf of language between them. Lovers have always been able to bridge this gap after a fashion of their own. Quickened looks and the touch of hands and lips can outrun the tongue now, as they did then. So Samuel Hadlock's vital presence came like a wind into that old house in Charlottenburg—a strong, salty wind, with a hint of spruce woods and untrodden snow from an arrogant, young world across the water.

And so, because he would not admit that they existed, he broke down all objections. Finally, in desperation, Ludwig Russ took a last stand: his daughter should only be married to an established householder. But he had not taken stock of this lover. Without more ado, Samuel Hadlock took his fortune in hand and bought a house. I have been told that it cost no less than ten thousand dollars, and if time has multiplied the sum, which is more than likely, at least it was considered a residence worthy of a magistrate's daughter.

It was characteristic of Hadlock that he should bend every energy he had, and lavish all his resources on the winning of Dorethea Albertina Wilhelmina Celeste. He had staked all he had three years before on his enterprise of showing the Esquimaux. He had succeeded, as he had expected to succeed. If it took his last dollar to make this young Prussian girl his wife, he would not hesitate to spend it. He knew he could make more. He always knew that. The Continent would be an even more profitable show ground than England had been. He was no longer merely a traveling exhibitor. He had a position to maintain, and he must live accordingly. He had bought the house to satisfy his future father-in-law, but he had no intention of settling himself in it. An attack of lavish spending had come upon him, and he now acquired a coach and pair of his own. He would travel in style and comfort with his wife beside him. His audiences would be altogether different from the country visitors to English fairs. Perhaps his visit to the royal gardens and palace at Potsdam had fired his ambition to attract the patronage of Kings and Queens; perhaps he wanted to show his future father-in-law that

God's Pocket

he could achieve as high a station as his own. At all events his scheme of living took a sudden spurt of magnificence. He had gone a long way from Cranberry Island, even farther than he himself guessed.

We only know it was on the twentieth of March, 1825, that the wedding took place. There is no hint from the neat German script of the yellowing certificate kept in his grandson's old trunk, of all that this amazing marriage meant, and was to mean to those two whom circumstance had flung together from such opposite poles. Translated into the bare English of such legal documents, it simply states that on that day the law acknowledged the union of "Captain Samuel Hadlock, Junior, of Mount Desert, North America, Capitalist, and Dorethea Albertina Wilhelmina Celeste Russ, daughter of Ludwig Russ of Hegermulthe, 'waltzer' of the Royal Brass Foundry at Charlottenburg, Prussia."

There is so much besides that one would like to know: if there was music and dancing in the house of Ludwig Russ; if the neighbors of Charlottenburg toasted the bride and groom as they drove away together; and if George, the Esquimau, attended his master, representing North America in his best native array. But it is all surmise. We are only sure of two things: that the little Prussian bride still lacked six months of her twenty-first birthday, while Hadlock had just reached his thirty-third year, and that from the day of their wedding he gave up trying to pronounce her name. Hannah Caroline was his choice, and so she remained for sixty years.

Chapter XIII

They shall enter into the king's palace.—Psalms.

BEFORE any other of the few relics of Samuel Hadlock's days of magnificence, except perhaps for the Journal itself, must come the gold snuffbox. It did not belong to old Sammy, having passed into the hands of cousins, the only other direct descendants of the Charlottenburg marriage. But the old man never could mention his grandfather without reference to it. The snuffbox seemed to have become more a family symbol, than merely an object of value. It was the tangible link between Cranberry Island and those fabulous personages whose palaces he visited in the months that followed his wedding.

It was in this same month of March, 1825, that he wrote briefly, but with extreme satisfaction, of his interview with King Frederick Augustus of Saxony. "I wass presented," he says, "with a buttifull Snuff Box of gold, value $300., from the King of Saxon. In this kind offes the King did not ofend me. I excibited on the water in the great gardin."

The entry is tantalizingly meager, despite its sly comment on the King's good manners and unpretentiousness. If he is correct in his date, it is surprising that he should have been giving his exhibition in Dresden, apparently less than a week after his own wedding. He may very well have made a mistake in the day, but it is hardly likely he would have set down the wrong month and year. No doubt the wedding was hastened because of this plan to open his show in Dresden. It was like him to combine business with a honeymoon. There is ground for the theory that the royal snuffbox may have been a wedding gift, but it has never seemed to me likely under the circumstances. The King of Prussia, in that case, would have been the natural giver of such a gift, since Ludwig Russ held so high a post in the Brass Foundry. A gold snuffbox would, it seems to me, have been a gift from one man to another, a gesture of royal appreciation for an afternoon's entertainment, presented much as a gold cigarette case might be today.

How Hadlock's audience with the King was arranged, and how his troupe came to the attention of Frederick Augustus I, he did not see fit to record. But the King appears to have had an eye for natural history and to have shown special interest in the stuffed specimens from northern waters. Undoubtedly, too, the arresting

On the 24th of March 1825
I Wass presented With a buitifull
Snuff Boxe of gold value $300.
the King of Sanon in this kind
Offer the king Did not afend me
I Exciteited on the watter in the
Great gardin whane i took $45 Dollar
in the furst day the Leckent Day 200
the thind Day 150 the fourth 95 Dollars
and finished with this town from
this to Prog in Ostnen Cuntrey Whare
I past through Sevrill Smell towns
Of little note the most Remarkable
Wone was the inoted town Cold
Tablites which is So remarkable
for its watters as thay are minorile
Watters and Iue buni most all
Sereses this place is Remarkable

God's Pocket

personality of their exhibitor appealed to the King. At that time he was an old man, nearing the end of his long reign, which had been a stormy one because of his part in the Napoleonic Wars. He had been first on the side of Prussia, but after the battle of Jena, he had joined forces with the French. After Waterloo he had suffered with others in the lost cause of Napoleon, though the Congress of Vienna had spared him his title and kingdom. He must have possessed uncommon powers of tact and wisdom, and have known how to mingle with all sorts of men. Certainly he could have had no more genuine tribute to his graciousness of manner than Samuel Hadlock's spontaneous "in this kind offes the King did not ofend me."

From the rest of this entry it appears that the King gave Hadlock the use of the palace gardens for an extended run. Business was excellent, and there seem to have been no competitors. Of his receipts, the Journal records: "I took $446 dollars in the furst day, the seckent day $200., the third day $150., the forth $36. and finished with this town."

So, having found that royal favor could be both pleasant and profitable, Samuel Hadlock set himself to win more honors in Prague and Vienna. He had not begrudged the weeks of determined wooing, but with courtship and marriage successfully achieved, he resumed his showmanship with gusto. Still heady with love, and spurred to greater effort by his realization

94

that he must provide Hannah Caroline with all and more of the luxuries she had been bred to, he launched into the most ambitious period of those four years. He had set himself up as a "capatalist from North America," and he must live up to the title. There can be little doubt but that he looked the part as he drove, with his young bride beside him, in his own coach along the roads of Central Europe. Darwin has said that "there is no such king as a sea-captain." He might have added "or a showman." Samuel Hadlock was both of these, and few men have been such absolute monarchs as he in his own particular world. He had found his place in the sun. If in his pride and vigor he grew too sure that it would always shine warmly upon him, it must be remembered that he was not born to walk humbly with fear in his heart.

Now that he was no longer dependent on stage or canal boat, and with Hannah Caroline's delicate charms to consider, he took the hundred-mile journey between Dresden and Prague with leisurely elegance. By this time he had grown accustomed to the sight of cultivated acres and vineyards; to ruined strongholds and castles and peak-gabled towns. A few months before he would have filled pages with descriptions of the country he passed through, but it was no longer a novelty. Besides he had a companion now to share his comments. The Journal was no longer his only outlet. Even in Teplitz, where they stopped, he only notes briefly that the place

God's Pocket

is visited in summer by the quality for its mineral waters, which, he adds, "due cure most all deseses." Watering places had become an old story to him.

They must have reached Prague sometime in April, and the fact that they stayed there till late May would indicate that the North American Exhibition prospered. But except for calling it "an old ancient town" and describing a remarkable bridge there, ornamented with life-size statues of Christ and the twelve Apostles and Daniel in the lions' den, and noting that "the tung spoken thare differs from all others on the Continent," Hadlock gives little hint of the impression it made upon him. What did, however, move him to fill several pages was the great Catholic celebration of the Feast Day of St. John of Nepomuk, which he witnessed with much amazement. With his flair for the miraculous he could not have selected a more fortunate time to be there. As in the case of St. Winifred he went to considerable pains to discover and recount the legend.

"The King of that plase," he writes, "haid one of the preists throd [thrown] off the Brig [bridge] about 500 years agoe becos he wood not confess to the King what his Wife had told him. He refused to inform him of hur privet matters. Tharefore he was hove off this Bridge and Dround." He goes on to tell how the priest was buried in the Cathedral, where his body still lies. "Everey hundred years," he continues, describing the miracle of the tongue, "the volt is opened . . . and his

96

tung is as good as ever and as fresh. The people from all partes of the Kingdome comes to behold the workes of god. The plase whare he lies is opened everey fifty years in order that the publick can see his fresh tung, for they are fond of tunges. The Presters [priests] takes out of a calf or cheap [sheep] one of thair tunges and plases it in the jois of that poor Skilington [skeleton] so to make the publick beleave that god has ordained this Mericle as a proof of his Ritchness [righteousness]. . . . This poor Devill was drounded about five hundred years agoe and to sopose his tung can never decay, whatta mericle. . . ."

There was certainly nothing of the mystic in Samuel Hadlock, who believed in letting poor devils and their bones lie undisturbed.

He goes on to describe the devout pilgrims who gathered from the whole countryside, some coming more than two hundred miles, and the rites he witnessed there on the sixteenth of May. "The presters colect his congergation to gether," he writes, "and march them along through the highway, Singing Sames [psalms] and holaring and baging the hole of the way. . . . Thay all lie on the bridge and in the streates for the spais of one weake . . . I was in prog about this time and saw all of the fun. Thare was so maney people that the poleas gives orders that no carige shood kum for fear of killing som of this sett [sect]. Som of them

God's Pocket

with read [red] stockins and cotes com down to thair neas and som with no stockins atoll."

Feeling perhaps that he could not cope with such religious competition, Hadlock packed his goods and set off towards the real objective of his tour. "Imbarked for vean [Vienna] in ostrige [Austria]," he begins his next paragraph. It is easy to account for his spelling of Vienna, when we realize that he wrote entirely from ear, and that the German "Wien" which he heard all about him, was a simple "Vean" to him. He clung to this form consistently, although he varied "Ostrige" in almost the next sentence. "Opened my Exerbition on the 12th of June," he notes, adding that "this is one of the finest townes on the Continent except Pariss. This cittey is formed by 4 townes jining to the main sittey."

It is strange to come upon such an entry as "This cittey is the Resedens of the Emper of Ostrey, allso the son of Boney, as the Emper is his Grandfather," and to remember that this was the young Duke of Reichstadt, then just entering his teens. To Samuel Hadlock he was a flesh-and-blood boy, not *l'Aiglon*, the tragic symbol of a lost cause.

At first reading of the Vienna entries, it seems surprising that the city should not have impressed him with its notorious life and gaiety. He mentions no cafés or places of amusement, although he made it his headquarters from June till late September. The probable explanation of this is that the famous capital had not

98

God's Pocket

recovered from the Napoleonic Wars. It had not yet struggled out of the depression and hard times which followed those years of invasion and foreign occupancy, and the Congress of Vienna, instead of helping the economic situation, had only intensified and prolonged the period of reconstruction. So we can only guess at the diversions he allowed himself in his spare time. We can only wonder what cafés and places of entertainment he visited, alone, or in company with Hannah Caroline.

There were several trips to places in the surrounding country,—one to Baden, a near-by watering place, which he found "buttifull," and the other to Pressburg, in Hungary, thirty miles distant. This particular jaunt was memorable for a calamity which befell one of his horses, for he notes that in crossing some river, with an undecipherable name, the animal "took kold, being so hott." This loss was a serious one and probably took more than his profits from the expedition. He had paid a hundred and fifty dollars for the horse, and besides losing this, he was obliged to sell the other and buy a new pair. For these two, which he mentions as being "large and stout from Poland," he had to pay three hundred dollars in cash. He makes no further comment on the price, but it is indicative of the value of good horse-flesh at that time. It shows, too, the hazards of such an enterprise as his; the unlooked-for disasters that accident, or a single act of carelessness, might produce. Even the most intrepid troupers on the road today

God's Pocket

would hardly have accepted such a setback with Hadlock's good grace.

He did not perform for the Emperor and Boney's young son, but he seems to have made an extensive tour of palaces and grounds. Both of the royal residences in Vienna and also the one in Laxenburg, met with his approval, and he pronounced them "most Butifull." It is significant, too, in view of later events, that he made special note of royal live stock. "He has allso," he writes of the Austrian Emperor, "a menagrey [menagerie] thair and plentey of fish in the pond of watter in the gardin." This hobby of collecting animal specimens which most kings of that time indulged in, evidently struck him as a good one. It may well have been in Dresden or Vienna or Munich that he first conceived the notion of bringing North American rarities to add to these royal museums of natural history. But this project was not to take shape in his mind till four years later.

100

Chapter XIV

I wear my hat as I please indoors or out.—WALT WHITMAN.

IT WAS September again, more than a year since Samuel Hadlock had set foot on the Continent; over three since he had left Big Cranberry. Even though he was a man little given to introspection, he must have marveled sometimes at how far his enterprise had taken him. By now that Maine island with its spare, wooden houses along the dirt road must have seemed almost stranger than the steep gables and cobbled streets of Europe, and the faces of his three children less familiar than those of the German boys and girls he passed. His own fortunes, from a comparatively small beginning, had expanded to unguessed proportions. Like a child's snowball that, gathering bulk and momentum as it rolls, suddenly becomes too much for one pair of hands to guide, so his own destiny was running away from him.

He did not know this as the expedition set off on the two hundred and fifty mile journey from Vienna to

101

Munich. He was concerned with plans and projects; pleased with the countryside; the good roads, and the pace of his new horses. It was vintage time. They climbed up hill and down, between such vineyards as have never flourished this side of the Atlantic. For several long bright days Hadlock and Hannah Caroline drove between these "wine mountans," as he called them, marveling at the vines trained against steep hillsides.

The fragrance of ripe grapes, hot in the sun, went to the head with a more potent intoxication than any stored in casks or bottles. There is only a single sentence in the Journal about this, but in it he managed to convey this subtle stirring of the senses. "The wine lookes most butifull," he writes, "when groing on the vines."

So the miles slipped away behind them. They were nearing Munich, or "Mintchin" as he spells the German "München." It was the season when summer and autumn are fused into one ruddy and golden whole, not so brief and brilliant as September in northern Maine, but a mingling of late flowers and early fruits that must have set Hadlock's naturally high spirits prancing. Perhaps unconsciously he felt that this time of lavish fruitfulness had its peculiar counterpart in him. Perhaps I only read this into the yellowing pages because I can look back upon his life, through the perspective of a hundred years, and see that the month of October, 1825, marked the peak of his magnificence. Money flowed into his hands and out of them as it had never flowed before. The North American Exhibition prospered, and at least six pair of royal eyes watched it with approval.

Fifteen miles outside the city the Hadlock coach stopped to visit the King of Bavaria's summer palace, and four miles farther on to inspect another which was noted for its collection of "fowles from all partes of the world." Here again was one of those natural history museums of live specimens which later on provided Hadlock with another enterprise. The ostrich seems to have taken his fancy, for he goes into a more than usually detailed description. "The ostrege," he writes, "standes 5 feat high. From the feat to the top of the head is 8 feat. The fethers is the finest in the world for ladies for thair hates [hats]."

Over the city itself he waxes immediately enthusiastic. "The houses is fine and large," he notes. "The Streates is broad and wall paved. The Side walks is paved with the finest stone and of diffrent collers of stones, and the Streates is kept remarkable clean." Outside the old walls he took many walks in "the Ditch" or low land, which had been turned into elaborate gardens. Of these the English Garden pleased him best. "All sortes of plantes are found groing in the senter of the gardin," he writes, "and thare is maney Inletts letting into the same." This was a place much to his liking.

Fortunately, the Munich entries seem to be complete

and we have a fairly clear idea of his impressions and activities there during a crowded fortnight. It was characteristic that he should have spent one of his first evenings at the theater. I like to think that Hannah Caroline went with him in her prettiest dress of shot silk or brocade, and that the big American, with his square shoulders and boldly cut features, and his small blonde companion drew many curious glances. But this was not for the Journal. We shall never know if they went together, or what spectacle unfolded before their eyes on the boards of that stage. It is strange to think that nothing remains of that night—not one of all that close-packed audience, from royal box to gallery; not the youngest dancer in the ballet; not a single musician bending to fiddle string or flute, is left to tell of it. All are gone as completely as the thousands of wax tapers that burned in the gold and crystal chandeliers. Only these faded scribblings from Samuel Hadlock's hurrying pen have survived, and these, by the merest thread of chance, lie here before me.

"The Grand Theator jines one part of the pallis," he writes. "This Theator is suposed to be the finest in the world. It has 6 tear of boxis all gilted from top to bottom. The boxis whare the King settes and the Royall famley is broilded with gold." There is a sumptuousness to boxes "gilted from top to bottom" and "broilded with gold," that Solomon in all his glory might have envied. It must have seemed a far cry to

God's Pocket

Hadlock from the tawdry, poorly lit stages of traveling show-troupes to this scene of larger spectacles, but he adapted himself easily to the change.

"The Senereyes inside," he goes on, "is butifully painted. The pilors of the building is polished stone. . . . On the 28th September I was at the play when the Royall famley entered the theater. The hous was crouded to execess. As the King and Royall famley made thair operans the Publick with one vois cried out long live thair noble King. When the King made 3 noble bous to the ordens, then the musick struck up god save the King. The entertainment was fine on that Evning in consequens of the King visiting the theater. The King opered to be mutch plesed. Loud clapes of aplais [applause] was heard during the evning. The specktators was about too thousen person, all apeared to be mutch plesed."

Less than three days from the time that Samuel Hadlock saw the King take his place in the Royal Box, he was making a personal appearance before him in the palace gardens. It was like him to move so fast from one event to another that even in the Journal he could not be bothered to set a period or a line of space between items. No one guessed, he least of all, that the kindly middle-aged monarch, Joseph Maximilian IV, who received him with such gracious informality, would be lying dead in his palace before Hadlock left on the next lap of his journey. The exhibition of North American curiosities must have been one of the last diversions he had on earth. But no one who watched the dexterity of the Esquimau as he cavorted and shot his darts from the canoe for the King's pleasure, had any inkling of tragedy or guessed how short the days were to be for both performer and royal patron.

All seems to have been particularly felicitous. Personal satisfaction lurks behind every letter of the entry that Samuel Hadlock set down. "On the 31st of September I Exhibited for his Majesty at his pallis in Nimphingburg [Nymphenburg] with the Ingin on the watter in his Gardin, when the Quean of Swedland was thair and the royall famley of the King. Thay seemed to be mutch plesed to see the maney manuvers on the watters with the Esquimaux. The Gardin is splendid. Thair is 2 fountans as large round as my bodey and osends 50 feate in the air. Thair the gratest founts in the world."

Two days later he was present at some races held annually where he saw the King present prizes, and where he comments upon "3 Inglish horses that outt runn the others one third." It was evidently the biggest day of the week's events, for he notes that "the number of Spectators was about 50,000. . . . All the fattest cattle and hoges and horses was thair," he adds, "and the King went round and vued them all. The finest and stouttest of its age the oners of itt drue a fine present from the King in order to incurage agracultur."

106

His next important performance took place on the fourth of October. "I preformed," he writes, "for the Rushish [Russian] imbasedor in the Inglish gardin of the King." News of the North American Exhibition seems to have been spreading in all circles, for at the same time he had established himself and the troupe in rooms at one of the best inns, where the show continued to do a thriving business. The earlier palace performance seems to have so pleased the King that he favored Hadlock with another visit, bringing royal guests with him on the last day of its run. "On the 7th of October," the Journal notes, "the King and Royall famley visited my Exibition in the black egle when the King seaid thatt he never saw sutch an Exibition in this town before. Allso the Quean of Swedland wass in kumpaney with them. The Kinges wife and the Kinges wife of Swedland are sister. Allso the Kinges Wife in Saxon is sister to the Kinges Wife in Bion. The Crown Prins in Prushia maired [married] one of the Kinges doutors of Bion. . . ."

Hadlock evidently made a determined effort to straighten out court relationships. That he often became involved is not surprising. Under the circumstances he did remarkably well, and it is interesting to set down the names of those he mentions here. King Joseph Maximilian IV, or Maximilian Joseph I, as Hadlock called him, brought his Queen, Caroline Maria Therese of Parma, while the Queen of Sweden, of

107

whom such special note is made, was the wife of one of Napoleon's generals, Bernadotte, who later became Charles XIV of Sweden. "The Kinges wife in Saxon" refers to Princess Marie Amelia, and the "Kinges wife in Bion" appears to have been Princess Augusta Amelia of Bavaria, while the Crown Prince of Prussia would have been Frederick William IV.

Even then he was not done with royalty. "On the 7th of October," he goes on to say, "I shott my Exibition in Mintchin, and ast the Quean [Caroline Maria Therese] for permition to preform in hir gardin at hir sumer palis. She redley offerd for that puorpus as all the other Kinges had dun the same." So on the following Sunday, the ninth of October, we find him being shown over the summer residence of the Queen and taking special note of its furnishings. By this time he had had plenty of experience in such matters. He was not to be taken in by gilding and veneer alone. It is pleasant to discover that he approved heartily not only of the Queen's taste in furniture, but of her orderly housekeeping. "I saw all hur firniture that wass butifull," he wrote. "The Chaires was all inlaid with silver and gold. All the beadstides and tables the same. The Roomes and firniture wass butifull and in the most neatest order."

Once more he was amazed at the vast greenhouses and at the "Menagerey of fowls," both filled with rare specimens from foreign parts, "pertickler from America." The great fish pond was a special wonder, and he mentions especially the tameness of the wild geese and swans. "Thay fead them with bread," he comments. "As you aproch the pond thay run to you soposing that you intend to fead them."

The whole surrounding countryside appears to have turned out for the next day's performance, and he surpassed all his previous records in the total receipts taken for a single showing. There could not have been a more ideal setting. The very incongruity of the formal gardens and the artificial lake waiting for the aquatic feature by a copper-colored native in full Indian regalia, must have added to the novelty of the scene. The day was particularly fair, and George appears to have been in fine fettle. "I preformed with the Indian on the watter in frunt of the Queans Pollis," Hadlock notes with a proud flourish. "The Spectators amounted to about 6000 . . . all seamed to be mutch pleased. The Indian turned himself bottom up severill times in his Canoe and with his dartes Dispatching sevrill geas."

Two days later Hadlock was back in Munich where he was able to witness an impressive celebration in honor of the King. The whole city, as well as the troops stationed there, all gathered in the cathedral to pay tribute to him, and formally to invest him with the title of Joseph Maximilian IV. He had been on the Bavarian throne for nearly twenty-five years and the ceremony ended with prayers that his reign might continue in

God's Pocket

health and prosperity. It was a strangely prophetic demonstration as the Journal records, "a mencoley (melancholy) ocorrance for the Citisons of mintchin." There is more than a mere reporting of a monarch's death in this first hand account that follows, for Samuel Hadlock had found special favor in the eyes of this King.

"On the 12th nite of October," he wrote, "the Rutchin imbasedor (Russian Ambassador) head a greatt Ball whare the King Joseph Mocksmillion of this Cittey was invited on account of the ministers leving the cuntrey for Rutchey [Russia]. After the King returned home to laxingburg to his pollis and went to bead he rung the Ball for the Servent. When the Servent entred the room he Discovred that one side of his magestes fais wass Black. He run down to give the alarm to the Kinges wife. On thair return thay found him Dead. The plais next morning operd like another town. The King wass greatley beloved by his Subjecks. That Daye on which he died wass the day on which he reseived the naim of Joseph Mack Million. The town all went to church to pray for him thatt he mite live long, the militerey allso. The number wass about 5000. All marched to the church and on thatt night he Died att 4 oclock in the morning."

The terseness and vigor of this statement of fact is somehow far more moving than if he had commented on the uncertainty of human life; than if he had waxed

110

eloquent about the blade of the grim reaper after the fashion of the day. But what he must have been thinking as he wrote, was that only a few days before he had been received by this King in his palace, and that they had talked together as man to man.

Chapter XV

Fame is a fickle food
Upon a shifting plate.
—EMILY DICKINSON.

THE Hadlock expedition rolled out of Munich on the morning of October 14th, leaving the city in a state of mourning. Stuttgart was to be the next objective, but there was a forced stop of two days at Augsburg because of an accident to the coach. "On my Jurney," Samuel Hadlock reports, "I brock the exeltre [axletree] of my cotch in the evning about 8 oclock in 2 mildes of Oxburg." This note throws some light on the strenuousness of their travel, for Augsburg lies thirty-nine miles from Munich, which was a long day's run for horses pulling the rather heavy coach needed for four or five people and their luggage. No doubt they started before daylight, and we have his word for it that they were on the road long after nightfall. Again there is no mention of Hannah Caroline, who must have felt the

112

strain of such arduous day's traveling, since she was to have a child in another five months.

She may well have welcomed the accident that gave them two days of leisure in Augsburg. At all events Hadlock seems to have taken it philosophically and to have devoted his time there to the Royal Art Gallery. How he learned that this old town, with its traditions of twelfth and sixteenth century commercial wealth, was also the center of German art, is a mystery. But he had a gift for discovering the special feature of each place he visited. With characteristic enthusiasm, he gave himself whole-heartedly to viewing art. His taste in old masters appears to have been catholic, though somewhat governed, it must be confessed, by the size of the canvas, the number of figures, and the amount of paint used.

"The next day," the Journal tells, "I went in the gallrey panting of the King. This paintinges is concidered to be the finest in the world. . . . Som 20 feate high and 25 brod. These peases is bin painted uperdes [upwards] of 1500 yeares. Som of them painted by the furst painters in the land." There follows a list of almost undecipherable names from which it is plain that this was no perfunctory visit. He was apparently much drawn to the Flemish Dutch School, since Van Dycks, and others are specifically mentioned. It is not at all surprising that the luxuriant canvases of Rubens should have made a strong appeal to his senses. But his listing of "Vinchies" shows, too, that he must have been impressed by at least one Leonardo. Of the collection of Holbeins, for which the gallery is famous, he has not a word to say.

It is particularly unfortunate that so many of the notes on Stuttgart, or "Stuckart," as he casually spells it, should be missing. It was finally reached on October 18th, after fifty more miles of driving. The stay there began prosperously enough. "The cuntrey round is fine," the Journal notes. "The Cittey lies in a hollor and sorounded by butifull hills covered with wine grapes of the furst quallitey." A royal performance was arranged, and Hadlock is soon commenting upon the next crowned head he exhibited before. This was William I of Württemberg, whose matrimonial history seems to have been quite notorious, for besides noting that he went before him in the Recruiting Saloon of the palace on October 24th, Hadlock adds: "The King is about 34 yeares of age, the Quean is about 25. This is the third wife thatt the King has head."

This is the last entry before Samuel Hadlock's fortunes began to dwindle. From the time he left Stuttgart, his luck took a sudden and violent downward turn. A later pair of scissors has cut out the pages that would give us the clue to some of the disasters that followed, particularly the explanation of George's unfortunate end. But we only know for certain, and this from a final entry many months later, that the trip between Stuttgart and Paris cost him four thousand dollars and much

God's Pocket

future profit in consequence of the "the Indian ding" (dying) in Strasbourg. He does not mention him by name, but there can be little doubt that it was George. He could have found another to wear the sealskin dress without much difficulty, and he would not definitely have said "the Indian" if it had been a later addition to the show.

In any case, my guess is as good as another's, and I believe that George's death may have been a violent one. All I have to go on is a single paragraph which joins what was evidently a long account on one of the missing pages. George, it seems to me from this, either got into trouble in some brawl, or else was taken with a fever which sent him suddenly out of his head. If it was the latter, as I am inclined to think it was, he probably appeared deranged and had to be confined in jail or some hospital.

"This was dun the nite before I saw him," the un-attached note reads. "When he came to himself he opered to be sorey for the ofens and Crime thatt he haid comitted there. Maid [mad] people som times are as sensable as aney people in the world att times and at other times no Devils half so bad as them . . ."

If this had been an entry about some incident in the town, it does not seem likely that Hadlock would have said so specifically "the nite before I saw him." It is also hard to believe that the reliable George, who had been through so many vicissitudes already, would have committed a crime without cause. The cause, I believe, was a sudden illness—perhaps the very same which overtook the King of Bavaria a few weeks before. But we shall never know any more than this. It may be that Hadlock's wise comment on the behavior of the mentally afflicted had nothing whatever to do with his own troupe.

Without further reference to the incident, the Journal continues. "This is the last day of my Exibition [December 1, 1825], in this town. I close tonite and leave after tomorough for Pariss, distans 220 mildes, which will take me seven days jurney. My Museum goes in the post van and costes me 2 dollars per hundred wate [weight]. And I goe in my one [own] cotch and horses."

In spite of loss and financial anxiety he was able to divert himself with sights and novelties of the countryside. There never seems to have been a time when reverses could keep him from taking note of all the diversity of human life about him. Once he had crossed the border into France, a new world of experience was at every hand. In a small town near Nancy his old passion for miracles was once more aroused by the strange case of a young girl whom "God has rote a singler work upon." It was a case of strange religious ardor, of the same legendary pattern that has been woven about Jeanne d'Arc, St. Elizabeth, and the Little Flower of Jesus. Hadlock probably knew nothing of such phenomena, but his curiosity was kindled by all that he heard of this French girl. He was fascinated by it as only a hard-headed man of affairs could be by the occult. So he devoted much space to this "young lady of 22 yeares" whose fame had already spread far and wide. He had apparently been skeptical of her powers until his stay in the town, where he made it a point to talk with many who knew her intimately and vouched for the truth of the stories.

"This girl," he begins, "when 3 and 4 years of age thay could nott keep hur out of the church. She was given to preing [praying] continley. At the age of 20 years she sweat blud at the ower [hour] of seven in the afternoon, and allso have the marks of our Savour in hur side and in hur feat. She has now kep hur bead [bed] for the last year and has not eat nor drunk for the last 9 montes [months]. Nor has hur lining [linen] bin shifted sens itt is white and clean as though itt haid bin putt on today. When she binges [begins] to sweat blud she apears in the gratest agonee. Thousens of people com to vissit hur and give hur money butt she will nott reserve aney of itt. This historey I beleved to be fals tell I com through this town and the hole of the Publick declard thatt itt wass thought thare is not the least dout about itt. Itt is none [known] in all cuntres [countries] to be fack [fact]. Thousens of people from most partes of this Kingdom has com to this plase to see the same. She is constently praing and talking about heven and the next world. Shee has bin putt in the jaill

117

to see if itt wass not fals aboutt hur eating, butt thay found itt through [true] and quitted hur."

But the affairs of the next world were not for Samuel Hadlock. "I then persuid my voige for Pariss," he writes. "On my way one of my horses got sick and I wass oblige to leave him behind and take post horses 50 mildes from Pariss." Troubles were coming on him thicker than hailstones, but he was still determined to set up what was left of his exhibit in the large room which he leased for show purposes "near the noted plais coled Palleroyal [Palais Royal]." It cost him 600 francs per month, or roughly something under a hundred and fifty dollars. The location, however, pleased him, and he adds with satisfaction, "Such another plais is not be found in the hole world as Palleralle."

Chapter XVI

Thou that hast a daughter . . . —William Allingham.

Of Paris, Samuel Hadlock wrote, "This Cittey is the most dissopated in the world." Unfortunately he did not follow up his statement with accounts of what he saw all about him. It is disappointing to have him so uncommunicative in his reactions to the French capital —the more so since he made it his headquarters from December, 1825, till April, 1826. Either his reverses on the journey there, the loss of George, and the failure to recoup the lost funds, kept him from his usual exuberant setting down of details, or else he was too occupied with new business schemes and concerned with the state of Hannah Caroline's health, to make many entries.

Although he still had the Museum of North American Specimens, it must have seemed a dull affair without a living Indian and aquatic maneuvers. So, like London, Paris remained indifferent to northern curiosities. Per-

119

God's Pocket

haps the trouble was with the times, for it was during the brief interval when Charles X, brother of Louis XVI, was reinstated on the throne which he was to lose five years later to the lumbering Louis-Philippe. If Hadlock made any attempt to go before this Bourbon King, there is no record of it, though he does observe that "the Kinges pallis is a splendid building and verey large and surpases the pallises in Germaney for grander and buttey."

One cannot help expecting descriptions of Notre Dame and the Champs Elysées, of Versailles, and the Louvre, but there are no references to them. The gory account of a murder fills part of a page. It appears to have been a rather sordid crime, of no special significance. Two robbers felled a bank clerk and made off with some fifty thousand francs. It was, however, the chief excitement of his stay, and though he was in no way involved, he noted it in the Journal. "I head nott bin in Pariss butt 4 dayes," he wrote, "then thare wass a horrid murder committ."

The Exchange he found "a fine building, none in the world to equal the same." The Boulevards, or "Boolwarkes," as he calls them, evidently proved a diversion, for he adds that there "the people can hardley pass for the croudes that has daley [daily] to pass that way." But for the Opera House, which must have seemed more dazzlingly "gilted and broilded" than the theater of Munich, he has not a word. Not a mention, either, is there of the stalls along the river, or of the Tuileries and the Luxembourg Gardens where he must surely have liked to walk and mingle with the crowds on fine afternoons. Although it was winter weather, there must have been Sundays warm enough for bands to play and children to ride on the Carrousel or gather before the timeless antics of puppets on their gay, high stages. He must have marveled before windows of fashionable shops on the Rue de Rivoli, where perhaps he bought a trinket for Hannah Caroline to wear. The newly installed gas lights that flared along the Boulevards and by every shop and café must have been an altogether new experience, and yet he did not bother to note them, as he had noted the sights of less fabulous cities.

Something of his old confidence and zest seems to have left him in these early months of 1826, as he faced new responsibilities for himself and his young wife, who waited for her confinement in a city that was as strange to her as it was to him. Hannah Caroline may have known a little French, as well as the English she had managed to pick up by this time. But the long lists of French words with their English equivalents, which he copied down in painstaking columns, are proof of Hadlock's own efforts to learn the language. One can only guess at the way this vocabulary may have sounded when rolled about on his State of Maine tongue. It was a practical list, and like the German one of a year and a half before, concerned chiefly with immediate, everyday needs. It is, however, significant that he should have made so sure of the French for "ice," "snow," "rain," "cloud," "iceberg," and "flat-ice" here in the center of European civilization. It was as if he always felt the north at his back; as if he could never be quite free of its magnetic influence. And so he learned to write *de la Neige* for "snow"; *mont de glace* for "iceberg," and *de la glace plat* for those wastes of flat ice he knew so well, and which were to have so strange a part in his fate.

Along with the word lists is the beginning of a letter to his parents, a fragment, evidently copied and finished on another sheet of paper. These few lines are in themselves meager, but his warm response to the long delayed news from home shows that family and Island ties were still strong in him.

Genuary 25th, 1826. Dear Father and Mother
I have just reseived your kind letters which has bin rote for 2 years and thay have gone all through Jerminey before thay reatch me after passing Ingland. . . .

How did he go on? What did he tell them of Hannah Caroline and his foreign marriage, of all his doings in those two years while the letters followed him all over Germany and Austria? Did he have messages to send to those three children on Cranberry Island who would soon be stepbrothers and stepsister to another Hadlock? One can only wonder.

God's Pocket

It is mid-March before the next entry, set down in evident haste and a hand that is less firm than usual. With pride and relief, but with as much terseness as if he were putting his customary "Dun Wall" after some particularly successful day's exhibiting, Samuel Hadlock wrote:

"March 16th Pariss, 1826. My wife gott to bead [bed] with a fine Doutor [daughter] at 10 oclock in the evning in the Streat Rue De Croson, Hotel number 12, near the Streat Clerey, And wass marid on Sunday the 20th of March in Prushey [Prussia] one year sens."

Without further comment on this highly important and personal event, he adds his last note written on foreign soil. It speaks for itself. "I shoot [shut] up my Excibition on the 20th March and solt [sold] the same up to oxion [auction] and did not sell for aneything, so I kepp it myself after lusing 4000 dollars with the same, traveling from Stuckartt to this Cittey, and the Indian ding [dying] in Strassburg. Now this ends my excibiting indians."

123

Chapter XVII

And now, all in my own countree,
I stood on the firm land.
— S. T. COLERIDGE.

IN LATE spring they crossed the Atlantic, and by the summer of 1826 they had reached the coast of Maine. There is no telling what vessel carried them; no way of knowing whether it was the port of Boston, New York, or Philadelphia, where they landed. There is not even a scrap of letter to give hint of Hannah Caroline's first impressions of the United States of America. Even though she was well broken by this time to shifting sojourns in unfamiliar cities of the Continent, and though her husband had sworn to bring her back to her people in a year or two, she must have known that it was a tremendous thing to turn her back on all that had been her world for twenty-two years. Did she feel, one wonders, sudden panic as she saw the trunks carried down to the wharves and knew that she would follow her

124

possessions across three thousand salty miles? Did she, perhaps, hide her face against Samuel Hadlock's great-coat as the last headland dwindled at the stern and the bows began to take those watery heights and hollows with the strange gait that no ocean traveler can ever forget once he has felt it under him? Or did she hurry below to their cabin and the demands of Jane Matilda, who already must have seemed to belong to the land they had not yet sighted?

Samuel Hadlock had chosen his daughter's name with an eye to the Island neighbors who would soon be saying it. He had had experience with foreign tongue-twisters and he made sure that hers should sound as plain and sensible as if she had not been born in Paris. Now that his show days were over, he shed them as easily as he had shed Cranberry Island four years before. He was eager to be back; to show his wife off in all her blond German beauty, and her dresses and bonnets and shawls of the latest fashion; to see his family and friends again and to be once more the center of the narrow Island stage. He was through exhibiting Indians, and for the moment he had not formulated any new enterprise. He still had some of his earnings saved, though recent losses and his lavish marriage arrangements had eaten into his capital. But there would be ways to make more; more ships to be built and fitted out in Cranberry Pool; more expeditions that he and his brothers would carry through to prosperous ends. Time enough to think of the next

God's Pocket

step when his feet were on familiar soil; when he had seen his three children again; when he had settled Hannah Caroline and their child in the new house he intended to build for her.

They probably made the next lap of their journey by one of the packet boats that plied between Boston and St. John, though they might have traveled by stagecoach from Bangor. But the water route is the more likely one. Coming down the New England coast, past Gloucester and the Isles of Shoals, they must have been in sight of low, rock-edged shores and marshy lands if summer winds prevailed and they need not nose through banks of fog. They would have stopped for cargo and passengers at Newburyport and busy Portsmouth; at Portland and Bath and Wiscasset. One can guess how Hadlock's spirits rose as he watched for old landmarks, and how he pointed out each one as it came into view. Now it was his turn to reel off difficult names for Hannah Caroline to repeat after him: the Piscataqua, Kennebec, and Androscoggin rivers; Merry-Meeting, Sheepscot, and Penobscot bays; Damariscotta, Woolwich, Monhegan, and Castine. One could hardly be learned before he was hailing another harbor or rocky headland.

After the populous shores of Europe, this coast line must have seemed fantastically wild and jagged to Hannah Caroline. Sometimes, at Bath and Wiscasset and Thomaston, there were clustered towns. But the wooden houses set high on those seaward bluffs must have looked new and flimsy to her after the solid stone and brick of continental seaports. Even though many were white and substantial, with high dormers and fanlight doorways that gave back the sun in sudden brightness, like specks of mica in a bowlder, the woods that had furnished their timbers still pressed close behind. The farther the packet sailed down that eastern coast, the smaller and fewer the settlements became; the more somber and impenetrable the ranks of thick-set green. This was Samuel Hadlock's own country. These dark harbors and rocky islands; these wild headlands with spurting surf at their bases; these bristling trees, sharp-tipped as Indian arrowheads against the sky; these scanty farms in half-cleared fields had all succored him. The bold, indomitable beauty of this place was in his blood and bone. The same fierce vigor of the marching trees animated him as he paced the deck beside her. Perhaps it frightened her to come suddenly face to face with his natural counterpart. Perhaps she felt only a renewal of that strange elation she had known when he strode into her father's house in Charlottenburg, bringing with him the freshness of a northern world. She had been married to him for nearly a year and a half, and their child slept in the cabin below, but until then she could never have quite known the man who was her husband.

I like to think that it was one of those incredible

summer mornings of hot sea-sunshine and a breeze with the faintest hint of ice in it, when they saw the hills of Mount Desert come up over the port bows, dim at first, like sea-bound whales, but gradually taking shape into the nine hump-backed hills that dominate sea and land for many miles. Champlain saw them so on a September morning in 1604 when he gave the island its name. Hannah Caroline must have followed Hadlock's pointing forefinger as he recognized one after another. Sargent, Green, Jordan, Western, Dog, Brown, and Flying, she heard him name them over, little guessing that she was never to be out of sight of those peaks as long as she lived.

Most coasting vessels, eastward bound, take a course outside the Cranberry Islands, since there are dangerous reefs to be skirted at low and half tide. Even now it takes skillful navigation and a knowledge of the waters to bring a fair-sized vessel close to shore. There was no lighthouse on Baker's Island then, and few beacons and buoys for guides when Samuel Hadlock returned from his travels. I have no doubt that if the weather was fair, Hadlock made it worth the packet captain's while to take the inner course to Mount Desert and set him and his wife and all their belongings ashore at Southwest Harbor. There he could get a friend's boat to take them across the Western Way to Big Cranberry. If they did this, Hannah Caroline would have had her first sight of her future home from the southwest, or seaward side.

God's Pocket

She would have seen a thickly wooded island, with rough, deeply indented shores, and perhaps the hulk of some old wreck tilted high on Deadman's Point. She must have wondered as they sailed closer, if it really could be inhabited, for she could not have seen the little harbor, the wharf, and straggling houses till they were well in, almost up to the entrance of Somes' Sound.

But whether they came from the west, or from the east and Frenchman's Bay, it is certain that they took the last few miles of their long journey in an open boat. It is not hard to picture them there among the piled-up trunks and bags, the bales of Arctic curiosities, with perhaps an incongruous Parisian bandbox or two. Unless it was unusually calm weather, dashes of spray must have spurted over the stout sides of that sloop or fishing smack, spattering Hannah Caroline's cashmere shawl and flowered leghorn, startling small Jane Matilda with salty welcome, while Samuel Hadlock laughed and let out more sail in his impatience to reach home.

And so they landed at the wooden wharf and climbed the long dirt road between the scattered boxlike houses where whole families of relations and neighbors came running out to meet Hadlock and his wife.

129

Chapter XVIII

*The gods are just, and of our pleasant vices
Make instruments to plague us.*
—SHAKESPEARE.

IF I had not set out to give a true account of Samuel
Hadlock, it would be simple enough to fill the next
chapters with possible doings, and to give a detailed recital of his return and the reception that was Hannah
Caroline's. But as it is, the actual happenings of these
next years are few and fragmentary. I do not even
know, for certain, what particular Island roof sheltered
them on their first night ashore. My guess is that they
went directly to stay with Hadlock's sister and his
brother-in-law, Samuel Spurling, though there may well
have been other visits to his father on Little Cranberry,
and to his four brothers, Elijah, Epps, Gilbert, and Edwin, who also had homes and families on one or the
other of the Islands.

But in spite of these nearer blood ties Hadlock seems
to have been more closely identified with Spurling than
with his own brothers. Mrs. Spurling was his only sister,

God's Pocket

and she had taken charge of his children after the death of his first wife. She had cared for them along with her own during those four years, and it was natural that her brother should have turned to her when it came to establishing his second household. Then, too, Samuel Hadlock and Samuel Spurling had much in common. Spurling seems to have had an even better right to the self-earned title of Captain than his more romantic brother-in-law, for he had had more vessels in his command. He was, in an entirely different way, the other most arresting personality of the Cranberry Islands of those days. He did not possess Hadlock's charm and amazing versatility, nor his power of expression, but when it came to courage and action, he was fully, if not more than, his equal. They had grown up together and as younger men had been associated in many expeditions by land and sea. On the Island he was even better thought of, probably because he was more steady and less overbearing than the other Samuel. He had nothing of his brother-in-law's volubility, and when a couple of years later he was in command of the Island-built schooner *Cashier* and with spectacular coolness broke up a nest of West Indian pirates, thereby winning a purse of gold and the thanks of the citizens of Trinidad de Cuba, his only comment on the affair was: "I just gave them a little bit of Hell, Maine style!"

But it was inevitable that the other Island women should have been critical of Samuel Hadlock's new wife.

131

God's Pocket

She must have been as much of a wonder to them as the North American curiosities had been to his audiences across the water. He had left with one exhibit and returned with another, even queerer one. They were all so closely related and intermarried that they could hardly have helped resenting the appearance of an outsider, even if she had come from Massachusetts or points south. They must have expected Samuel Hadlock to remarry, but undoubtedly they had counted on his selecting another State of Maine wife, one cut after their own pattern, who talked as they talked; who dressed as they dressed, and who vied with them in quilting and preserving. Hannah Caroline's youth and delicate beauty, exaggerated by the inappropriate elegance of her dress, must have galled them for many months. Later they came to know and admire her, to do for her in times of illness and disaster as they would for other neighbors; but they never let her forget where she hailed from. She was always "The Prooshan Lady," and even today I have seldom heard her referred to by any other name. It was the penalty, I suppose, that all foreigners paid in the days before easy transportation and commercial development changed the self-sufficient order of such small communities.

Her being married to Samuel Hadlock could not have helped matters, for once the excitement of his return had subsided, and his stories of continental grandeur had lost their first novelty and begun to wear a little thin,

132

the neighbors must have grown impatient of the airs he gave them both. Hannah Caroline herself seems to have been modest and simple enough. She liked her sister-in-law, and she made friends with her stepchildren. She had pleasant manners and a genuine desire to please, rather than to impress, these women. But her husband made no attempt to hide his admiration of her. He boasted openly of her superiority on all occasions, and if he had brought home a princess for his wife he could not have taken more pride in her. Indeed, with his sense of the dramatic, he was given to enlarging upon their romantic love match until her comfortable, slightly more than middle-class family became nothing less than minor royalty, and she herself related to practically every crowned head in Europe. Every now and again I have heard her referred to in vaguely royal terms, proving that the legend he created still persists. He could not have done otherwise, though it must have made her Island transplanting more difficult. Love, for him, was too tremendous and complete a passion to be hidden under a blanket. Hannah Caroline was his, and so she became the embodiment of every grace and virtue. It could not have helped irritating the feminine portion of Big and Little Cranberry to see how he doted on this small, blonde girl; parading her before them in her latest finery, treating her as if she were some rare parlor ornament, too delicate for the ordinary uses of kitchen and pantry.

God's Pocket

Pride and love in Samuel Hadlock were so interwoven that he could not, had it occurred to him to want to, separate one from the other. Like the gold snuffbox, that he could never resist exhibiting whether the occasion warranted it or not, she had become another symbol of his achievements across the Atlantic. So it was natural that he must set her up in a new house; in a larger and more expensive one than any other that had yet been built on the Island.

Samuel Spurling happened to be at home between voyages, and he undoubtedly helped. The only clue I have been able to find in this matter of the house building, is a single mention in some old papers that came to light several years ago in a Little Cranberry Island attic. One of these is a record of money paid on lumber and other building materials in Samuel Spurling's name. The date is 1826 and tallies with the time of Hadlock's return, so it seems reasonable that the two men handled it between them. They both had money tied up in several vessels and evidently in the past and during the next few years did business together. The house which resulted from this, if my theory is right, was built about a mile up the road from the wharf at the southwesterly end of Big Cranberry. It has passed through many hands since then, and has suffered various remodelings. But even this, and neglect in the last twenty years have not quite spoiled it. Long before I knew its history, I could never pass it without noticing the wooden dignity

134

of its lines. It stands with the usual lilac bushes between it and the road, and an old apple tree or two behind. A steep field slopes from the back door down to the same cove where old Sammy first told me the story, where he worked his small garden on land that no longer belonged to his family. Even without later enlargements, it must have had several more rooms than any other Cranberry house, and there are hints of good paneling and a simple, well-made doorway to bear out the Hadlock tradition. He must have had all the available men in the neighborhood working on it, and though it cost considerably less than the house in Charlottenburg, Samuel Hadlock put all the money he had left into it, and probably borrowed some beside from Spurling and his father.

For the next months, probably well into the following winter, this absorbed him completely. He was a man who could turn his hand to anything, and once the heavy work of building had been accomplished, I have no doubt that he did much of the finishing and fitting by himself. Samuel Taylor, the oldest son of his first marriage, may have helped at odd jobs, for he was a likely boy of twelve at the time of his father's return. His daughter Sally had been seven when he left, and now she was eleven, at the edge of her teens. Smith Cobb had grown into a sturdy seven-year-old from the baby he remembered. They must have seemed hardly his own children to Hadlock, more like his Spurling nephews and nieces, as he watched them playing with the new baby in her cradle; introducing their young stepmother to cranberry picking, fish-drying, and other Island ways in which she was so strangely lacking. These three belonged to another man. They were part of a life he could never quite fit into again after the four expansive years away from home.

Lavishness had grown on him. Along with ambition and self-esteem it had become a necessity. Once the new house was built, he could not settle down in it. He was obsessed by the old restlessness and desire to be cock-of-the-walk. His own easy-going, pleasant vices had trapped him. He was poorer than he had been before he set out on his travels, and now he had acquired tastes far beyond the simple Island ones he had known. His wife might have adapted herself to humbler ways, but his pride would not let her. To find himself suddenly cramped for money was a new experience after the last years of free-handed spending. It was not in his nature to count the pence when he could make dollars by the hundreds and thousands as he had lately proved. Already he was beginning to cast about in his mind for the most likely way to recoup his fortunes. And while he turned over the various schemes that stirred in his active brain, the Islanders were watching. The other Hadlocks, as well as the Stanleys and Bunkers, the Gilleys and Gotts, the Spurlings and Hamors and Bulgers all gave him grudging admiration. But at the same time they undoubtedly felt that he was sailing rather too close to the wind just then.

"God Almighty's overcoat wouldn't do to make Sam Hadlock a vest!" they must have said to one another plenty of times during those next years.

Chapter XIX

Muse not that I thus suddenly proceed;
For what I will, I will, and there's an end.
—SHAKESPEARE.

IN TELLING me of this part of their story, old Sammy always spoke harshly of his grandfather. It was the only time I ever heard him critical of the Hadlock side of his family.

"Grandfather was something of a villain," he used to say. "He promised to take her back home to see her folks, and he never did."

In this, chance and many other circumstances were against him. But there is no denying that he was something of a villain. Lucifer himself could not have been a more disturbing element in Paradise before the Fall, than Samuel Hadlock before he began to assemble his next expedition.

Jane Matilda had hardly passed her first birthday the

138

following March before the whole Island knew that there would soon be another young Hadlock to fill her cradle. The return to Germany which Hannah Caroline must have been cherishing could not be undertaken for another year at least. The new baby was born towards the end of September, 1827, just at the season of cranberry gathering and the equinoctial storm. It was a very different affair from the one in Paris a year and a half before; but Mrs. Stanley, who lived on Fish Point by Cranberry Pool, and who was midwife for all the scattered island women, seems to have managed well with her own primitive resources. At all events, this second child was a boy, and his father once more did the christening. He named him Epps, and wrote it down in full on an unused page of the Journal with a fine flourish to the capital E and H. It was a family name of English origin that had been repeated in many generations of Hadlocks.

It must have been a busy winter for Hannah Caroline with two small children and a house to care for, and with her husband pressed for ready money. Samuel Spurling may have been away again on another voyage, for it was the next year that he had the sensational brush with the pirates off Cuba, and so the two sisters-in-law probably combined their households. In any case Mrs. Spurling lent a hand in her brother's home, and there may have been a bound-out girl, or some neighbor's half-grown daughter to help. There is not usually a great fall of snow on these seaward islands, but the winters are long and severe, with gales of sleet, bitter winds and giant seas on the outer ledges. Even today when most boats are equipped with engines, winter is a slack time, with frequent spells when fishing is too difficult and boats are sometimes frozen in for days on end. No one starves in a place so near the sea, and there is plenty of wood to burn; but the fare grows monotonous and the days and nights are one long round of keeping fires up and the kettle boiling. Charlottenburg and all the snug comforts and luxuries of her father's house must have seemed sometimes like a mockery to Hannah Caroline. But she was twenty-three and married to the six-foot showman who had swept her off her feet on that other cold winter morning. They were still romantically in love, and his easy hopefulness and magnetism could get the better of even her most homesick moods.

During that winter Samuel Hadlock busied himself in various ways. He helped in the refitting of one of his father's vessels that was laid up in the Pool for overhauling, and he also worked in his own barn stuffing seals. Along with his other accomplishments he had somewhere picked up a knowledge of taxidermy. Seals had been plentiful in the near-by waters all the summer before, and he had shot a number of fine ones. These skins he cured and stuffed and mounted himself, remembering those he had seen abroad in various royal museums he had visited. He had talked with the King of

English	Francais
God	le monde, entier
Spurut	le Diable
heven	le ciel
Conjurer	conjurer
Sun	le soleil
Moon	la lune
Star	l'étoile
fire	le feu
water	l'eau
Erth	to terre
Air wind	l'air le vent
cloud	un nuage
Rain	De la pluie
Snow	De la neige
icebarg	Mount de glace
flat ice	De la glace platte
aurora borealis	l'été
Summer	Le jour

God's Pocket

Saxony and several of his important patrons about these specimens and had found them interested in this sort of thing. He was clever at keeping the lifelike attitude of animals, and as he worked it occurred to him that here was his next scheme for making money. Those palaces he had been shown through in Vienna and Prague, in Dresden and the various kingdoms of Germany, all went in for such collections. He had seen them himself, and he knew that nowhere had there been such seals as his. If it had been comparatively simple to show his North American Exhibition to Kings and Queens, it would be equally easy to sell them stuffed seals from the arctic. Live human specimens were a risky proposition. They might get drunk, or fall sick, or even die, as he knew from his own experience. But here was something sure and profitable if he could only carry it through on a large enough scale.

To have an idea that tickled the romantic as well as the practical in him, was more than enough for Samuel Hadlock; so before it was spring again and the ice fairly melted in the wagon ruts he was making plans. It took him most of that spring and the following summer and fall to get them under way, and at first no one would take him seriously. It was not an unusual thing for a man to take the summer off sealing in the North. Hadlock and other Island men had done this several times before. But they had sold the furs at trading posts for the flat price that the skins would bring. This notion of getting seals to stuff and sell to foreign kings for fabulous sums was just another of Sam Hadlock's pipe-dreams. He had, of course, carried out the other one of exhibiting the Esquimaux, but no one on Cranberry could see that it had brought him much besides a wife who was only just learning their ways; some knick-knacks from far parts, and a lot of wild ideas that certainly did him no good when it came to settling down. The older men and women shrugged and thought he would get over this latest notion, but as time went on more and more of his cronies and the younger men of the Island began to listen to him.

From the first Hannah Caroline was out of sympathy with the new scheme. She hated to see her husband going out to the barn to work. The idea of stuffed seals was repugnant to her, not only physically, but because it meant of necessity another year or more of delay before the promised return to Prussia. It seems to have been the only time in their life together when she openly took sides against him. She had let him name her children what he wished. She had tried to conform to his wishes and to his people's idea of what a wife should be. She loved him more even than in the days of their continental prosperity, but this separation and delay was something she could not face. Perhaps her love for him gave her some peculiar inner warning. Instinctive dread may have laid a chill finger on her heart as she pleaded with him to give up the plan.

But she might as well have argued with the twelve-foot tide that swept into the Pool twice a day. His mind

143

was made up, and he was bending all the energy he possessed to carrying out his new scheme. Gradually his enthusiasm infected most of the younger men thereabouts, and he began to collect his crew. Under the spell of his glowing pictures and the magnetism he could always summon, he persuaded his father, the older Samuel Hadlock, to let him have the *Minerva* for the trip. He raised what cash he could and agreed to pay the rest out of profits of the voyage. Several of the other men took shares in her and his father personally saw to her overhauling.

The *Minerva* had been built in Cranberry Pool eight years before, and had been half owned by Bunkers and other Mount Desert men at the time of her launching. They probably still owned their part when Hadlock fitted her out to "go down to the ice after seals." On an old bill of sale, miraculously preserved, she appears to have been a two-masted schooner, a little over sixty feet long, of about seventy-five tons, with one deck, a "square stern, no galliries, no figure head."

She seems a small vessel for the crew of seventeen men that Samuel Hadlock had collected to go with him to the north. In the records the number is given as nineteen, but this is because he took fourteen-and-a-half-year-old Samuel Taylor along for his first sea voyage. There is no complete list of the company, and besides father and son I can name only four others who went. One was William Gilley, an enterprising Island man in his early twenties; Joseph Stanley, the son of John

144

Stanley and his French wife, Marguerite La Croix, who were among the first to settle on Little Cranberry; Ellis Kingsbury, part owner of a store on Fish Point by the Pool; and Joseph Ober of Mount Desert. The story goes that the other thirteen were all from the islands and near-by harbors.

By March of 1829 the *Minerva* was ready to set off. For weeks past there had been little talk of anything else on Big and Little Cranberry and the larger island of Mount Desert. Samuel Hadlock was in his element again. The ring of confidence and authority was in his voice as he issued orders and held forth before admiring groups wherever he went. His chin was in the air and his feet more high-stepping than ever as he went about the business of their departure. The old exuberant optimism swept all before him, charging the whole Island with the current of a human dynamo. Hannah Caroline must have long since realized the futility of her pleas. Perhaps even she became infected with his enthusiasm as she helped in his last preparations, sewing on the buttons of his shirts, collecting his handkerchiefs, and working his initials in the corners with stitches she had learned in far-off Prussia. It would not be a long trip, he assured her, only eight months or so. But she must have guessed that that meant a year, maybe longer.

And then the morning came, fine and sunny, with a stirring of spring in the keen air. There were still patches of thin snow under the spruces; the hills across the Western Way wore their woods like winter fur;

ice crackled in the ruts on the shady side of the road, but herring weirs and traps were out alongshore, and on neighboring Sutton Island men were working in a newly cleared field. It was high tide and every dory and skiff pushing out with men for the *Minerva*, a sturdy, brown shape that dominated the nearer waters. The wooden wharf was crowded with women and children, and eyes looked from every seaward window.

Hannah Caroline must have watched with the rest, knowing that she had no power to stay the sails that men were already unreefing. She could make out the figures of her husband and young Sam in one of the boats pulling alongside the schooner. There was the creaking of anchor ropes, and more new canvas spread out in sharp relief. Then she heard cries across the water, shouted good-byes that met and mingled and went by her on the crisp salt air. Her eyes blurred suddenly, even as they strained. Some one lifted up the little girl at her skirts, and some one else took the little boy from her arms and set him shoulder-high to see his father sail.

146

Chapter XX

For hope is but the dream of those that wake!—MATTHEW PRIOR.

WHEN they could no longer see the *Minerva's* topsails standing out to sea beyond Bunker's Ledge and the easterly islands, the women went back to their kitchens, and the older men and boys to their boats. The Vernal Equinox was almost upon them. Spring would come with a rush, and after that the bright, brief days of a northern summer would set in.

Hannah Caroline was busy as she had never been in all her twenty-four years. Whatever the other Island women may have said of her at first, they all gave her credit now for being a capable wife and mother. They might smile at her love of finery, but they admitted that she kept her house clean and her children well fed and tidy. The sealing expedition had made a bond between them. There was hardly a household there or on Little Cranberry that was not personally linked to the *Mi-*

nerva. Even those from which no husband or son or brother had gone, were connected by marriage with some member of the crew. Samuel Hadlock, as the sponsor and organizer of this new enterprise, had found favor with them again, and his young wife became their charge. The men remembered her when they had a good catch of fish, or if they killed a sheep or a pig. She had no man now to do for her, and they helped her with a garden patch in odd spells of leisure. Her charm and youthful beauty and her tricks of speech and dress were appealing. Perhaps the women guessed that if Sam Hadlock's wife had been plain she would not have been so much on the men's minds. But even so, they admitted her ability. She was spunky, and she did not sit back and take on as might have been expected.

"Beauty doesn't make the pot boil," was never said of her in those long months of waiting.

She had need of all her German thrift as time went on and the first September frost touched swamp maples to scarlet and turned birches to as bright a gold as the King of Saxony's snuffbox. She must have taken it down sometimes from its place on some shelf out of reach of her children's mischievous fingers, remembering the carefree first months of her marriage; the easy luxury of the show days in Dresden and Vienna and Munich; and the comfort of her father's house in Charlottenburg. An ironical souvenir it must have seemed to her as she polished it on her apron and felt the smoothness of the gold under her hands that were hardening to unfamiliar tasks. There was the Journal, too, with the names of cities she had known set down in her husband's bold writing. There was his silhouette in the black frame with the brass mountings, his shadowed features that she knew by heart.

Perhaps there were occasional letters from home that came by long and devious routes, and sometimes she may have been able to send back answers in the German script that was beginning to seem strange to her for lack of use. But there was no chance of word from the north, no possible way of sending even a message to the captain of the schooner *Minerva*.

No one on the Island had really expected the expedition to be back in eight months. When November passed, they all knew that meant she would be laid up all winter in the ice. Cold weather, they pointed out, was a time to stay frozen in the ice and Samuel Hadlock knew the arctic too well to take foolhardy risks. Some fine spring morning, or by early summer at the latest, they would see the *Minerva* bearing down the Eastern Way under full press of sail.

But when August came in again they began to wonder and speculate among themselves. They made excuses to Hannah Caroline, but by another Christmas, at the edge of 1831, they admitted that something must have gone wrong. They told her all the stories they could of other delayed voyages. They explained in painstaking detail accidents that had forced vessels to put in at remote parts of the world for many months while their crews repaired damage. The desolate coast of Greenland in any but the brief summer season would be a particularly difficult spot to patch a ship if any harm had come to it. Lumber was scarce, and they could wait for months without sighting another vessel. But Samuel Hadlock would be able to find a way out of even so serious a situation as this. He was resourceful in any emergency. She must have listened to them and tried to believe they were right.

By another spring everyone in the region began to express openly the fear that had been kept back before. The elder Hadlock and his sons, along with Samuel Spurling and other seafaring men, combed the news that every coasting packet could bring, searching for some word from the north. Accounts of the *Minerva* and the sealing expedition were sent to newspapers in Boston and other seaports in the hope that some ship coming from Greenland might be able to shed light on the mystery. But none reported sighting her, and it was nearly three years since she had put out.

The strain of waiting was beginning to tell on them all, though they clung tenaciously to what hope they could muster. Hannah Caroline was twenty-seven now. Jane Matilda was six, Epps Hadlock nearly five, and neither could remember their father. Sally and Smith Cobb helped their stepmother about the place. But getting along without a man to fish and cut wood and do the heavy work was growing more and more difficult. The Hadlock father and brothers helped, and the Spurling family shared all they had. They were kind, but Hannah Caroline was too high-spirited not to know that she was a burden to them. Every day she must look out across the Western Way where she had seen Samuel Hadlock cross so often in an open boat; she must see his coat with the bands of fur, hanging on its peg in the entry; the compass and charts he had left behind in their accustomed places. Above all, she must have come to dread passing the rough barn where he had been so busy stuffing the seals that were still there in the boxes he had made for them.

Chapter XXI

At one stride comes the dark.—S. T. COLERIDGE.

AND then, more than four years after the *Minerva* had set out, word came of her captain's fate. It was brought direct by another Maine man, Captain Stanley of neighboring Northeast Harbor, on his return from northern waters. He had been on the lookout for any news of the earlier expedition, but nothing could have been stranger than that a chance encounter with some Esquimaux should have revealed it to him. Samuel Hadlock's enterprises had always bound him to the north. George and Mamie Megunticook had shared his high days of adventure across the Atlantic. It was curiously in keeping with the past that he should have returned to meet his end in their white world of ice and snow. This is the story Captain Stanley brought back.

He had gone ashore with men from his vessel in a remote part of Greenland. They were hunting seals

152

when they fell in with a party of Esquimaux. Several of them could speak a little English and one of their number carried a gun. This caught the Maine captain's eye, and as he looked, he was startled to recognize Samuel Hadlock's name on the butt. He questioned the natives, who told him of the *Minerva*. Their description of her and her captain and crew tallied perfectly, and the time was the winter after her departure. She had been frozen fast in the ice-pan for many months while her men hunted seals. They had good luck and a full shipload of skins, but they lingered, waiting for warmer weather and an open passage. Though they had such a fine cargo aboard, the captain still wanted more. Then, late in the day, he sighted a particularly handsome seal which he determined to have. With his gun in hand, he set out after it alone. It had seemed near, but he had to follow it far across the ice.

Darkness was coming on and in a few minutes, one of those sudden, blinding snowstorms set in. It caught him before he could turn back and the men on his ship were powerless to go to his aid. As soon as it was light next day the Esquimaux went with them to search for their captain. They found him kneeling on one knee, his gun raised in the act of taking aim—frozen dead.

The Esquimaux helped them to tie a heavy weight to his ankles; to cut a hole in the ice and lower Samuel Hadlock's body into the dark pocket. His gun and a handkerchief that had belonged to the dead man were given to one of them at that time. As soon as it was possible for the ship to get clear of the ice, the other men had taken her out. That was all they could tell.

To this day it is all that anyone knows of the schooner *Minerva*. Not one of the nineteen souls aboard her ever came back. Her fate, like her captain's, belongs to the far north, to shifting ice floes and hidden reefs, to the looming peaks of ice whose name he once learned to write in French.

No such single tragedy, before or since, has ever touched the Cranberry Isles. There was hardly a household to which the news did not bring personal loss. Many refused to believe that the rest of the men would not return. On Little Cranberry, Joseph Stanley's mother continued for years to keep the traditional lighted lamp at the window on stormy nights to guide her son back. Clarissa Gott, who had been married to William Gilley only two months before the sailing, and a dozen other Island women hoped against hope. But for Hannah Caroline there was grim certainty.

Captain Stanley had brought her proof from the north. It was not the gun, but her husband's handkerchief that he put in her hands. The initials that her needle had worked there still showed on the square of linen. Nothing could have seemed more bitter than that this flimsy bit of cloth should have come back to her. It had survived him after the tragic fashion of personal possessions.

The neighbors, stricken as they themselves were, rallied about her. The lay minister, Ebenezer Eaton of Mount Desert, came to bring her Divine comfort, and compose a sorrowful garland of verses commemorating her loss and young Clarissa Gilley's. He had a gift for poetry and he did his best. But stark disaster such as this must forever elude rhyme. There are older Island women today who can sing the long, sad stanzas through to the end. The words have even been put between covers. But they have never moved me as old Sammy did by his more personal recital of his grandmother's grief.

Everyone expected the Prussian Lady to break down. But she did not become crazed with grief or express her woe in foreign accents. They might have known better how to cope with such conventional lament.

"She didn't cry or take on after they told her," old Sammy used to say. "She went right out and borrowed a horse and wagon and got a boy to help her load those seals onto it. She drove right down to the shore and dumped 'em in the water."

All the way along the Island road they reasoned with her. They reminded her that Samuel Hadlock had stuffed them with his own hands; that they were a valuable legacy and would bring good money. But no argument could move her. Her blue eyes were dry and wide as she went on past the groups of horrified neighbors. There was a sudden set look to her young face that kept them at a distance. Even the boy, who may have been her stepson, dared not protest as they got the first load down to the water. It was hard work for a woman and a half-grown boy to do between them. The wooden cases were heavy and awkward to handle. She must have grown panting and red-cheeked from exertion, her fair hair roughened in the sea wind as she urged the horse back for the second load.

All those years of waiting she could not bring herself to touch or even look at the boxed seals. But now she would get rid of them. They must not stay in the barn another night. She had known with instinctive premonition, as she had seen him bending over them, that they would do him hurt. She had known and she had been powerless to turn him from them. They were as hateful to her as if his very blood were spattered on the new pine planks. She moved like some sure, mechanical figure of a woman, straining and pushing; sitting straight and tense on the high seat of the creaking wagon; leading the horse back again and again up the steep mile of road. Later on there would be bitter nights of resentment and remembrance. There would be sighs for the sweetness of lost days and nights together in foreign cities; sudden gusts of tears as she folded his greatcoat, or woke alone in the bed where he had once lain warm beside her. But on that day she was possessed by a single thought. The seals in their neat cases were somehow responsible. They had taken him away from her forever. Only a woman in despair could have been so sure and unreasoning.

That was how Hannah Caroline spent the remaining hours of the day the news came. She did not pause for food or drink till the barn was emptied. She did not answer her children when they ran to her, or stood whimpering on the doorstep. It was only when the last box had splashed into the water by the wharf, and she saw the tide taking them all out to sea that she could give herself up to sorrow. Then she could send the boy back with the borrowed horse and wagon. She could stop to speak to her scandalized neighbors, and take her children by the hand once more.

Old Sammy never was able to understand her gesture. But to me it is cruelly plain. He always ended with regret that she should so wantonly have destroyed his grandfather's last handiwork in her first shock of grief. It was some satisfaction to him that a coasting packet from St. John, passing shortly after, should have fished up one of the bobbing cases from the waters of the Western Way. They took it to Boston and the seal was given a place of honor in the old Museum, where it was on exhibition till fire took it years later. So Samuel Hadlock's ambition was realized after all, in spite of the Arctic and Hannah Caroline. Fate saw to it that he had the last word.

157

Postscript

THE story is finished, but one cannot dismiss the Prussian Lady, left a widow at twenty-nine, and accounted the prettiest woman on the Islands. It would have been natural for her to go back to her own people; to take her children home to Charlottenburg and the life she had known there; to resume the Dorethea Albertina Wilhelmina Celeste of her young days, now that Samuel Hadlock need no longer balk at such a musical string of names. But she lived on for fifty-two years, never out of sight of the Mount Desert hills and the rugged shores where she had taken root. She was Hannah Caroline to the day of her death. Her children grew up like the other Cranberry boys and girls, with only the fairer skin and bluer eyes of their German inheritance to mark them as hers.

Perhaps she planned to go back at first. But there was no ready money to draw on. A man could have managed it. He could have worked his way on some coasting vessel to Boston and then on another to the Continent. But for a woman and two children without resources it was difficult, well-nigh impossible. It would have taken months for her to send word of her loss and to get an answer from home. Money, if it reached her at all, would have had to be entrusted to some reliable captain or traveler, and even if it was safely carried across the Atlantic it might have taken months or even years to be delivered to such an out-of-the-way spot as Big Cranberry. According to old Sammy's story, her father died soon after the arctic tragedy, and by the time she might have returned, the close family ties were broken.

So she did the only thing that a lone woman in such a place could do. She found another man to marry. In March, 1839, ten years after the *Minerva* sailed for the north, she became the wife of Andrew Haines of Southwest Harbor, just across the Western Way. She was a woman nearly thirty-five then, a capable one, well broken to the ways of an Island housewife. Only her fair Teutonic beauty, her slight foreign accent, and her love of feminine finery betrayed her among the other Maine women. She bore three children to her second husband, and was an exemplary wife and mother. But her life was like a book in two volumes. All the incredible chapters of youthful adventure, of romance and ardent love, of despair and high tragedy had been crowded into the first part.

I suppose that the memory of Samuel Hadlock dwindled in time to her. Yet, like the flat, dark outlines of the silhouette, his shadow must always have lain on her heart. Though she lived to be past eighty, and died at the edge of another century, she kept the gold snuffbox, the yellowing Journals and the other mementoes close at hand. She saw her children grow up and marry, but there was always a special bond between her and the daughter born of her early love in far-off Paris.

Jane Matilda ran true to Island traditions, marrying twice and living for many years in the house her father had built on Big Cranberry. It was there that her son, the old Sammy that I knew, grew up. It was on that same land that he spent the last years of his life in the little cabin by the Back Cove. He was her only surviving child, and to him she bequeathed the Journal, the silhouette, and most of the other souvenirs of the North American Exhibition. The gold snuffbox went to Epps Hadlock, who took it with him to another part of the state. His children were daughters, so although there are many Hadlocks on Big and Little Cranberry today, no direct descendants of Samuel Jr., carry on the family name. Old Sammy was never quite reconciled to this. But he made up for the lack as time went on by a reverent absorption in the past, until, for him, it became more important than his own narrow present, and the glamorous personality of his Grandfather Hadlock as true and compelling as the compass needle that points to the magnetic north.

The following verses, attributed to the pen of Ebenezer Eaton of Mount Desert who preached the funeral sermon, I have set down in full, not so much because they are significant as native poetry or folklore, but because the Hadlock legend would not be complete without them. They were printed in a broadside, of which several copies are still in existence. Nothing could have been less characteristic of Hannah Caroline than these lines which a well-meaning preacher put into her mouth.

THE LOSS OF THE SCHOONER MINERVA

Oh, Thou who reignest enthroned on high,
Who canst our wayward thought control,
Who art to all Thy creatures nigh,
Oh, calm the anguish of my soul.

Thy deep designs are good and wise,
Though not to thoughtless mortals known;
They are concealed from mortal eyes,
By clouds and darkness round Thy throne.

I would not of Thy will complain,
Nor e'er a murmuring thought impart;
But, oh, I can't conceal the pain,
That deeply penetrates my heart.

Although I still have friends most dear,
And greatly do I prize their love,
Yet there was one more truly near,
And valued far the rest above.

We, firmly joined in wedlock's bands,
More firmly still by friendship's ties,
Had joined our hearts as well as hands,
And dreamed of future years to rise.

God's Pocket

But, ah, how shall I tell the tale?
In four short years our joys are o'er.
My briny tears can naught avail,
Nor from the deep my friend restore.

In winter's stern, relentless reign,
When fiercely howls the raging storm,
My husband dared the northern main,
Where fields of ice the seas deform.

A hidden rock or mountain wave,
Or crashing ice with fury borne,
Has brought him to an early grave,
And from my arms my husband torn.

For of his vessel's numerous crew,
Not one remains to tell their fate,
No one alive the moment knows
That closed at once their mortal state.

Of nineteen seamen who set sail,
Not one shall meet his dear friends more,
While many lonely widows wail
And orphans, too, their loss deplore.

That crew must end their voyage there,
No human arm could lend them aid,
No eye could see the death-bed where
Beneath the deep their bones are laid.

Long will the sea its motions keep
Fathoms above their coral bed,

162

But none shall wake them from their sleep,
Till the last trump shall wake the dead.

All day my mind oppressed with grief,
Laments my loss with ceaseless sighs,
And evening brings me no relief,
In dreams I see his image rise.

Far from my parents and my home,
With my loved husband did I stray.
We did through distant Europe roam,
And o'er the Atlantic find our way.

And though upon this western shore,
I've many friends both true and kind,
Yet none can that lost one restore,
For whom I left my native land.

Oh, Thou who art the widow's friend,
And who for us did bleed and die,
To me Thy grace in trouble lend
And show Thyself a helper nigh.

Like all funeral wreaths, it is less enduring than the remembered jest, the scribbled word, and the proud step that can persist through a hundred changing years.

Afterword

The events upon which *God's Pocket* is based took place between 1820 and 1830, and the book was published over one hundred years later, in 1934. Recent research at the Library of Congress confirms that there was a papoose and that Sam Hadlock, Jr., showed his little troup in New York City and perhaps in other East coast cities, before sailing with George and Mary Coonnanock to Europe in 1822.

An item in the February 7, 1821, issue of the *New York Commercial Advertiser* states that Captain Hadlock had shown his "Esquimaux Indians" to many thousands of persons and "much curiosity has been excited." The story goes on to state a suspicion that "Hadlock has taken these poor creatures from their country, and brought them to a land of strangers, contrary to their inclinations." A Moravian missionary interviewed the Eskimos and called the matter to the attention of the mayor of New York, who held a hearing and ordered Hadlock brought to trial. Hadlock was cleared when it was found that George could speak English.

The same New York newspaper reported the late February death of the "Infant Esquimaux" and, on November 11, 1821, published a letter from Labrador confirming that the Eskimos had indeed accompanied Hadlock voluntarily. The papoose had been removed from Hadlock's custody at the time of its death.

The story tells us that Hadlock spent about four years in Europe and then returned to Great Cranberry Island with his German bride who became known locally as the "Proosian Lady." He sailed again for the Arctic in 1829 — ostensibly to obtain fresh specimens of Arctic animals for a new show. One can't help but wonder if he wasn't also seeking another Eskimo family?

Hadlock and his crew were not heard from for four years. Then, in 1833, his rifle was spotted in the hands of a group of Eskimos who, when questioned, reported that he had frozen to death while hunting on the ice. Could, perhaps, the real story have been a bit different? Perhaps the Eskimos got their retribution for Hadlock's failure to return the little family as he had promised.

Hugh L. Dwelley, President
Islesford Historical Society
June 1999